GLUTEN-FREE BAKING MADE SIMPLE

GLUTEN-FREE BAKING MADE SIMPLE

Properly delicious recipes for every day

CHERIE LYDEN
Founder of wholegreen bakery

murdoch books
Sydney | London

INTRODUCTION *7*
MY KITCHEN ESSENTIALS *11*
MY PANTRY ESSENTIALS *12*
FLOUR BLENDS *15*
NOTES ON INGREDIENTS *16*
GENERAL BAKING TIPS *17*

PART *ONE*

sweet

MUFFINS *20*
CUPCAKES, SLICES and SCONES *38*
BISCUITS *58*
FRUIT CRUMBLES, PANCAKES and CRÊPES *70*
LOAVES *82*
CAKES *92*
PASTRY, TARTS and PIES *114*

PART *TWO*

savoury

MUFFINS *134*
SCONES and PANCAKES *148*
PASTRY, QUICHES and PIES *160*

PART *THREE*

bread

BRIOCHE and BUNS *184*
FOCACCIA, FLATBREADS and LOAVES *202*

THANK YOU *216*
ABOUT THE AUTHOR *217*
INDEX *218*

INTRODUCTION

'Let food be thy medicine and medicine be thy food.'
Hippocrates

I'm so pleased that you have picked up this book. The pages that follow are the result of years of hard work and dedication to create delicious gluten-free baked goods for those who suffer from coeliac disease or need to eat a gluten-free diet for whatever reason, and they are something of which I'm extremely proud.

But the beginnings of this book – and the development of my business, the Wholegreen Bakery – are also the result of a personal health journey. A few years ago, both my youngest daughter Lucia and I were diagnosed with coeliac disease (mine not full-blown, only latent), while I was also diagnosed with hypothyroidism and Lucia with a similar condition called Hashimoto's disease. Autoimmune conditions run on both sides of my family, so we were bound to get something somewhere along the way! While my husband and eldest daughter Holly do not have any autoimmune conditions (well, at least not for the moment) both Lucia and I now eat a strict gluten-free diet, as this is the only treatment for coeliac disease.

On receiving Lucia's diagnosis, I wanted to ensure that she had access to healthy and delicious gluten-free food such as good bread and pastries, as well as the occasional sweet treat. This was, in part, due to my background as a trained nutritionist (which had given me a good understanding of the importance of diet in contributing to health) but also a result of my upbringing. Growing up in New Zealand as a child to Tongan and Dutch parents, a love of food was imprinted on me in early childhood; my mother's family always came together over a feast and all my early happy memories revolve around food – the eating of it, for sure, but also the preparation, whether through the everyday baking of things like banana bread to use up the bananas that were going black, the making of coconut milk from scratch or the preparing of dinner for the many aunties, uncles and cousins who inevitably turned up every night at my grandparents' house expecting to be fed! Cooking in our house was a way to share love, and I wanted to make sure Lucia didn't miss out on these experiences just because her diet was, necessarily, more limited.

So I began to dip my toes into the world of gluten-free baking – which should come as little surprise, I suppose, as baking runs in the family. My grandfather was a baker and wooed my grandmother with fresh loaves of bread! What did surprise me, though, was what exactly this brave new world looked like. Gluten-free products were hard to find, and the quality of those that did exist was lacking when it came to the most important things: taste and deliciousness. And how can you make anyone happy without those?

The gluten-free recipes out there that I could find were also, to my mind, pretty hit and miss, so I experimented, tested and trialled various options until I had developed food that I was happy with and proud to have cooked, and it was at this point that I saw the opportunity to open the Wholegreen Bakery and spread that message into the wider community. (After all, if my daughter and I were facing this challenge to find delicious gluten-free baking, then surely others were too?) In the years since, it has been such a joy to see the business grow and thrive and the word spread, and to be a part of bringing the pleasure of eating back for so many people who thought that certain foods – like a good croissant, a decent loaf of bread or a delicious savoury (or sweet) tart – were no longer options for them. It's an extremely humbling and rewarding experience to hear that you've changed someone's life by giving them back the food they love to eat.

I hope the tried-and-well-tested recipes contained within the pages that follow will arm you with the confidence you need to get into the kitchen and create for yourselves the baked goods that you might otherwise miss out on. They are filled with the knowledge I have picked up over my years of gluten-free baking, including all the tips and techniques you need to achieve excellent results. More than that, though, they are a collection of foods you'll want to eat and share with *everyone* you love, regardless of whether they have intolerances or dietary restrictions, simply because they are – first and foremost – delicious. And, really, that's what good food is all about, isn't it?

Happy baking!

MY KITCHEN ESSENTIALS

Having the right tools in the kitchen makes baking so much easier. I prefer to see the following tools as a baking investment rather than an expense. Sure, you could possibly do without some of them, at a pinch, but do you really want to compromise your gluten-free baking journey before you've even started?

- Apron
- Bamboo proving basket (perfect for bread)
- Biscuit cutters
- Bread knife
- Brownie/slice tray (a good universal size)
- Cake stand (to show your cakes off!)
- Cranked spatula (for icing cakes)
- Cooking knives
- Different-sized cake tins (and a mix of deep and shallow, to suit your needs)
- Different-sized mixing bowls
- Dutch oven/heavy cast-iron casserole dish with a lid (for baking bread)
- Flat baking trays (for biscuits, pies, quiches)
- Food processor (great for doughs, breadcrumbs)
- Good-sized chopping board

- Grater (with both fine and coarse sides)
- Hand mixer (you'll need this if you don't invest in a stand mixer)
- Ice-cream scoop (spring-loaded)
- Loaf tin (for cakes and bread)
- Measuring spoons and cups
- Microplane
- Muffin tins (in both small ½ cup and large 1 cup indentation sizes for both muffins and cupcakes)
- Non-stick crêpe pan
- Non-stick frying pan (large size)
- Oven mitts
- Oven thermometer
- Pastry brush
- Pie tins (in both individual and family sizes)
- Quiche tins with removable bases (in both individual and family sizes)

- Rolling pin
- Ruler
- Scales
- Scissors
- Small serrated knife
- Spatula (for folding and for scraping the sides of the bowl)
- Stand mixer with a whisk, paddle and dough hook attachment (investing in this means you won't need a hand mixer)
- Strainer (2–3 different sizes, to use as a sieve when sifting)
- Tea towels
- Texta or pen
- Timer
- Whisk (for most of your mixing)
- Wire racks (for cooling)
- Wooden spoon
- Zester (to make long strips of zest for decorating)

MY PANTRY ESSENTIALS

These essentials are the ingredients I have in my pantry and are what I use when making the recipes in this book. Yes, there are other gluten-free flours, starches, sugars, oils, nuts and seeds out there, so don't feel bound by this list alone and do please stock the ingredients you prefer to use. The ones listed here are my favourites and (most importantly) are the ones I know the whole family will enjoy.

GLUTEN-FREE FLOURS

plain (all-purpose; see page 15 for recipe)
self-raising (see page 15 for recipe)
white rice flour
brown rice flour
coconut flour
white teff flour
chickpea flour

GLUTEN-FREE STARCHES

corn-derived genuine maize/corn starch (cornflour)
potato starch

FLAKES

quinoa flakes

RAISING AGENTS

baking powder (gluten-free)
bicarbonate of soda
instant dry yeast

GUMS

xanthan gum
guar gum
psyllium husk powder

GRANULATED SUGARS

caster (superfine) sugar
icing (confectioners') sugar (gluten-free)
raw sugar
brown sugar

LIQUID SUGARS

honey
rice syrup
golden syrup

OILS

sunflower oil (or other light-tasting oil such as vegetable or rapeseed)
olive oil (light-tasting)
coconut oil

CHOCOLATE

cocoa powder
dark chocolate (minimum 54% cocoa solids)
white chocolate

SPICES & FLAVOURINGS

ground nutmeg
ground cassia or cinnamon
ground cardamom
ground ginger
vanilla extract
vanilla paste
salt and cracked black pepper

DRIED FRUITS

currants
sultanas
raisins

NUTS

almonds
hazelnuts
pecans
walnuts

NUT MEALS

almond meal
hazelnut meal

SEEDS

chia seeds
sesame seeds

MISCELLANEOUS

baking paper
aluminium foil
paper towels
plastic wrap

FLOUR BLENDS

Plain Flour

MAKES APPROXIMATELY 1 KG (2 LB 4 OZ)

850 g (1 lb 14 oz) brown rice flour

100 g (3½ oz) potato starch

50 g (1¾ oz) gluten-free cornflour
(cornstarch)

7 g (⅛ oz) xanthan gum

STORAGE
Store in an airtight container in a
cool dry place for up to 3 months.

This plain (all-purpose) flour blend should become your go-to for
almost all the gluten-free baking within this book. The ingredients
are easily available (either online or in the gluten-free section of
your supermarket or health food store), though just be sure that the
cornflour you are purchasing is derived from corn and not wheat
(as you'll find some are). Because of the high ratio of brown rice
flour to starch, I find this flour blend to be consistent in my baking,
especially compared to a lot of the supermarket gluten-free blends,
which are often high in starch and low in rice flour.

I like to use brown rice flour here as it's more wholesome and
results in moister baked products than white rice flour, which I find
to be quite drying. In this cookbook, when I refer to plain flour it
is to this blend with the xanthan gum included – the xanthan gum
helps with your bake's texture and creates lightness and elasticity,
as well as preventing the pastry from crumbling. If you need a blend
that's gum-free for whatever reason, simply omit it.

Sift all the ingredients together into a large mixing bowl, then whisk
together well to ensure they are well mixed.

Self-Raising Flour

MAKES APPROXIMATELY 1 KG (2 LB 4 OZ)

850 g (1 lb 14 oz) brown rice flour

100 g (3½ oz) potato starch

50 g (1¾ oz) gluten-free cornflour
(cornstarch)

55 g (2 oz) gluten-free
baking powder

7 g (⅛ oz) xanthan gum

STORAGE
Store in an airtight container in a
cool dry place for up to 3 months.

For a good self-raising flour blend, all you need is a good plain
(all-purpose) flour blend to which you add gluten-free baking
powder in order to make it self-raising. This is the blend I refer to
in this cookbook and it is the same as my plain flour blend above,
with the starches creating lightness in the flour and counteracting
the brown rice flour's natural heaviness. Simply omit the xanthan
gum for a gum-free recipe and be sure to search out gluten-free
baking powder that is specifically labelled as such, as many baking
powders are derived from wheat.

Sift all the ingredients together into a large mixing bowl, then whisk
together well to ensure they are well mixed.

NOTES ON INGREDIENTS

CHIA SEEDS

Chia seeds are superstars of the gluten-free baking world – made into a gel, they help to bring lightness to your baking, which is pretty much the holy grail. They are either black or white. I tend to use whatever I can get my hands on, though the white are less likely to stand out in food; if you are after the most aesthetically pleasing result then choose these.

DARK CHOCOLATE

I like to use dark chocolate with a minimum of 54% cacao solids in my baking, as it's more intense and less sweet than milk chocolate or regular dark chocolate with a lower cacao content. While I do use chips occasionally, I often prefer to break chocolate into rough chunks (particularly for my muffins), as I think it makes the bakes look more rustic and the irregular size of the pieces make for more interesting eating. Ensure to avoid products which contain malt barley. For those with lactose intolerances, dairy-free dark chocolate can be found in supermarkets, health stores and online.

FROZEN BERRIES

I always have frozen berries on hand just in case I can't get the fresh berries I need that day or when out of season – they're easy to find in the shops all year round and are a great thing to have in the kitchen. If using frozen berries in your baking, be sure to keep them frozen right up until you need them. If you let them defrost, they will leak their juices into the batter and change its colour.

DAIRY AND NON-DAIRY EQUIVALENTS

While I often use butter and full-fat regular milk in my baking, I'm aware that many people who have complications with eating gluten also suffer from lactose intolerances. The recipes contained within these pages will all work well with whatever milk or butter alternative you choose, so please feel free to replace the milk with lactose-free, almond, macadamia or gluten-free soy alternatives and the butter with vegan butter, your favourite dairy-free butter option or a light oil… whatever you prefer!

XANTHAN GUM

Xanthan gum helps to provide lightness and creates the perfect crumb for your gluten-free baked goods. My plain and self-raising flour mixes include xanthan gum for this reason, but if you are using a pre-bought flour mix then I suggest checking to see whether xanthan is included and then adding 1 teaspoon to 300 g (10½ oz) flour if it isn't. Check and see how the bake turns out and adjust with a little more (or less) the next time around as needed.

GENERAL BAKING TIPS

CREAMING BUTTER AND SUGAR

Creaming butter and sugar together is an important first step in many of the recipes in this book – it brings air into the mixture, helping to leaven your baked goods and create a tender crumb. The softer your butter, the quicker your butter and sugar will become pale and cream together. (This is especially the case when using non-dairy butter.) Be careful not to over-cream, as this will give your bakes a dense, gluey texture.

DON'T OVERWORK YOUR BATTER

With all baking, but particularly with gluten-free baking, you want to be careful not to overwork your batter when making up muffin and cake mixes. If the recipe says to mix everything together until 'just combined' then do stop there. A lumpy batter is often absolutely okay – in the oven the ingredients will combine and you'll end up with a great end result, whereas if you overwork it you'll end up with a gummy, or unpleasantly chewy, bake.

HOW TO CHECK YOUR BAKE IS READY

There's nothing worse than a dry, overcooked bake. While it does take a bit of practice to know exactly when you've reached the right point to take it out of the oven, there are a few things you should be looking for:

1. The sides of the cake should be just starting to pull away from the tin.

2. The middle of the cake should feel springy and pillowy if you gently press your finger against it.

3. A thin skewer inserted into the centre of the cake should come out clean or with a moist crumb and not covered in streaks of wet, uncooked batter. If all the above are good, then you can be pretty sure your bake is ready.

UNIFORM SIZING – AND COOKING!

It could come from running a bakery, but it's very important to me that the baked goods I make are all of a nice, uniform size! There are a few reasons for this – not only is it more aesthetically pleasing to see a group of evenly sized muffins or cookies arranged together, but those muffins or cookies will also bake uniformly, reducing the likelihood of inconsistencies. To ensure this is the case with muffins or cupcakes I like to use a No.16-size spring-loaded ice-cream scoop (which equals ¼ cup) to load up the tin, with 2 scoops for muffins and 1 scoop for cupcakes – I have found this to be by far the cleanest and easiest way to scoop up muffin mix and guarantee a consistent result.

PART *ONE*
sweet

MUFFINS
20

CUPCAKES, SLICES and SCONES
38

BISCUITS
58

FRUIT CRUMBLES, PANCAKES and CRÊPES
70

LOAVES
82

CAKES
92

PASTRY, TARTS and PIES
114

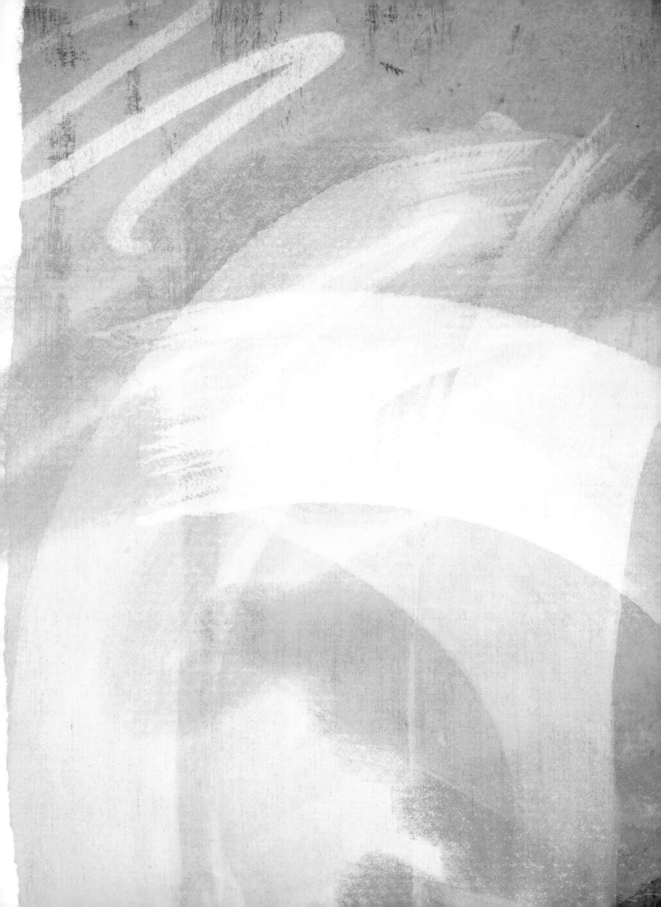

MUFFINS

Muffins are a baking staple of mine and for good reason.
Individually portioned, they can be whipped up quickly when
they're needed, they're flavoursome and simple to make
and – most importantly – the whole family loves them.

20–37

Blueberry, Apple and Lemon Muffins

MAKES 6 LARGE MUFFINS

Two much-loved classic fruits are elevated with a zing of citrus in this failproof recipe. These sweet muffins are a mainstay of ours at home, ideal for the kids to take to school or demolish after.

1 tablespoon chia seeds

¼ cup (60 ml/2 fl oz) boiling water

2 eggs

½ cup (125 ml/4 fl oz) light oil
(e.g. sunflower, rice bran,
canola, light olive oil) or
melted butter

1 cup (250 ml/9 fl oz) milk (or
non-dairy alternative)

1⅔ cups (275 g/9¾ oz)
gluten-free self-raising flour
(see page 15 for recipe)

¼ teaspoon bicarbonate of soda
(baking soda), sifted

½ cup (100 g/3½ oz) brown sugar

½ teaspoon ground cinnamon

1¼ cups (200 g/7 oz) fresh or
frozen blueberries, plus extra
to decorate

¾ cup (150 g/5½ oz) grated
apple, plus extra apple slices
to decorate

finely grated zest of 1 lemon

Preheat the oven to 190°C/375°F (170°C/325°F fan-forced) with the oven rack positioned in the middle of the oven.

Line a large 6-hole muffin tin with high-sided muffin wraps (or grease the tin with a little butter or oil if not using papers).

Mix the chia seeds and boiling water together in a small bowl. Set aside for 2–3 minutes to form a gel.

Whisk the eggs, oil and milk together in a separate bowl. Tip in the chia gel and whisk again to break up the gel. Set aside.

Add the dry ingredients to a large bowl and whisk well to combine.

Using a spatula, tip the wet mix into the dry mix and gently fold it through until just mixed. (The mix should still be lumpy.) Fold in the blueberries, apple and lemon zest.

Using a ¼ cup spring-loaded ice-cream scoop, take a flat scoop of mixture and empty it into a muffin wrap. Repeat the process so you have two scoops per muffin wrap. (The mix should be about two-thirds of the way up each muffin wrap, leaving enough room for the muffins to rise.)

Decorate the top of each muffin with a couple of slices of apple and a few blueberries, transfer to the oven and bake for approximately 20 minutes, then rotate the tray and continue to bake for a further 10 minutes, or until the muffins are lightly golden and a skewer inserted into the centre of each comes out clean.

Remove the muffins from the oven and leave to cool in the tin for 10 minutes before turning out onto a wire rack. Serve warm or at room temperature.

STORAGE

These muffins will keep stored in an airtight container in the refrigerator for up to 3 days, or in the freezer for up to 1 month.

TIPS

- Removing the muffins from their tin to cool completely prevents the muffins sweating in the tin and going soggy.
- If your grated apple turns brown, it will make no difference to the end result. If using frozen blueberries, keep them frozen until needed. That way they won't defrost and turn your batter purple.

Banana, Ricotta and Honey Muffins

MAKES 6 LARGE MUFFINS

These are perfect for breakfast on the weekend or any time you find yourself with overripe bananas – they'll help make the muffins wonderfully sweet and moist.

1 tablespoon chia seeds

¼ cup (60 ml/2 fl oz) boiling water

2 ripe to overripe bananas, mashed, plus extra banana slices to decorate

2 eggs

½ cup (125 ml/4 fl oz) light oil (e.g. sunflower, rice bran, canola, light olive oil) or melted butter

1 cup (250 ml/9 fl oz) milk (or non-dairy alternative)

1⅔ cups (275 g/9¾ oz) gluten-free self-raising flour (see page 15 for recipe)

¼ teaspoon bicarbonate of soda (baking soda), sifted

⅓ cup (60 g/2¼ oz) brown sugar

½ teaspoon ground cinnamon

½ cup (115 g/4 oz) fresh ricotta, plus extra to decorate

¼ cup (90 g/3¼ oz) honey, plus extra to decorate

STORAGE

These muffins will keep stored in an airtight container in the refrigerator for up to 3 days, or in the freezer for up to 1 month.

Preheat the oven to 190°C/375°F (170°C/325°F fan-forced) with the oven rack positioned in the middle of the oven.

Line a large 6-hole muffin tin with high-sided muffin wraps (or grease the tin with a little butter or oil if not using papers).

Mix the chia seeds and boiling water together in a small bowl. Set aside for 2–3 minutes to form a gel.

Whisk the mashed banana, eggs, oil and milk together in a separate bowl. Tip in the chia gel and whisk again to break up the gel. Set aside.

Add the dry ingredients to a large bowl and whisk well to combine.

Using a spatula, tip the wet mix into the dry mix and gently fold it through until just mixed. (The mix should still be lumpy.) Add the ricotta and honey and gently fold in, being careful to break up the ricotta only slightly with your spatula.

Using a ¼ cup spring-loaded ice-cream scoop, take a flat scoop of mixture and empty it into a muffin wrap. Repeat the process so you have two scoops per muffin wrap. (The mix should be about two-thirds of the way up the muffin wrap, leaving enough room for the muffins to rise.)

Decorate the top of each muffin with a couple of slices of banana, a few small ricotta chunks and a little drizzle of honey, transfer to the oven and bake for approximately 20 minutes, then rotate the tray and continue to bake for a further 10 minutes, or until the muffins are lightly golden and a skewer inserted into the centre of each comes out clean.

Remove the muffins from the oven and leave to cool in the tin for 10 minutes before turning out onto a wire rack. Serve warm or at room temperature.

TIPS
- The riper your banana, the sweeter and moister your muffins will be. Using a very ripe banana as decoration will result in a more caramelised end result.
- If using frozen overripe bananas, be sure to defrost them completely before using, otherwise the mix will be too cold and won't rise properly.

AT WHOLEGREEN BAKERY WE ARE PASSIONATE ABOUT MAKING TRULY DELICIOUS HANDMADE GLUTEN FREE BAKED GOODS, USING FRESH SEASONAL INGREDIENTS AND NO PRESERVATIVES.

Raspberry, White Chocolate and Coconut Muffins

MAKES 6 LARGE MUFFINS

Try this recipe in summer when raspberries are in season and don't cost the earth (though if you can't wait, you can easily use frozen). The tartness of the raspberries and the sweetness of the white chocolate complement each other perfectly, while the coconut flakes give the muffins texture.

1 tablespoon chia seeds

¼ cup (60 ml/2 fl oz) boiling water

2 eggs

½ cup (125 ml/4 fl oz) light oil (e.g. sunflower, rice bran, canola, light olive oil) or melted butter

1 cup (250 ml/9 fl oz) milk (or non-dairy alternative)

1⅔ cups (275 g/9¾ oz) gluten-free self-raising flour (see page 15 for recipe)

¼ teaspoon bicarbonate of soda (baking soda), sifted

½ cup (100 g/3½ oz) brown sugar

½ teaspoon ground cinnamon

1¼ cup (155 g/5½ oz) fresh or frozen raspberries, plus extra to decorate

75 g (2¾ oz) white chocolate, cut into small chunks, plus extra to decorate

⅓ cup (20 g/¾ oz) coconut flakes, plus extra to decorate

Preheat the oven to 190°C/375°F (170°C/325°F fan-forced) with the oven rack positioned in the middle of the oven.

Line a large 6-hole muffin tin with high-sided muffin wraps (or grease the tin with a little butter or oil if not using papers).

Mix the chia seeds and boiling water together in a small bowl. Set aside for 2–3 minutes to form a gel.

Whisk the eggs, oil and milk together in a separate bowl. Tip in the chia gel and whisk again to break up the gel. Set aside.

Add the dry ingredients to a large bowl and whisk well to combine.

Using a spatula, tip the wet mix into the dry mix and gently fold it through until just mixed. (The mix should still be lumpy.) Fold in the raspberries, white chocolate and coconut.

Using a ¼ cup spring-loaded ice-cream scoop, take a flat scoop of mixture and empty it into a muffin wrap. Repeat the process so you have two scoops per muffin wrap. (The mix should be about two-thirds of the way up each muffin wrap, leaving enough room for the muffins to rise.)

Decorate the top of each muffin with a few coconut flakes, a couple of raspberries and another chunk or two of white chocolate, transfer to the oven and bake for approximately 20 minutes, then rotate the tray and continue to bake for a further 10 minutes, or until the muffins are lightly golden and a skewer inserted into the centre of each comes out clean.

Remove the muffins from the oven and leave to cool in the tin for 10 minutes before turning out onto a wire rack. Serve warm or at room temperature.

STORAGE

These muffins will keep stored in an airtight container in the refrigerator for up to 3 days, or in the freezer for up to 1 month.

TIPS

- Coconut flakes give these muffins texture and crunch. You can substitute shredded coconut if you like, but I think the coconut flakes look better. Desiccated coconut, on the other hand, will change the texture of the muffin quite a bit – the mix will be drier, and the end result will be a little on the heavy side.
- If using frozen raspberries, keep in the freezer until needed. That way they won't defrost and turn your batter pink.

Pear, Dark Chocolate and Walnut Muffins

MAKES 6 LARGE MUFFINS

Pear and dark chocolate – need I say more? And you don't have to go super fancy here; just a block of dark choccy from your pantry or the supermarket will do. Walnuts add a lovely crunch and make the muffins more filling.

1 tablespoon chia seeds

¼ cup (60 ml/2 fl oz) boiling water

2 eggs

½ cup (125 ml/4 fl oz) light oil (e.g. sunflower, rice bran, canola, light olive oil) or melted butter

1 cup (250 ml/9 fl oz) milk (or non-dairy alternative)

1⅔ cups (275 g/9¾ oz) gluten-free self-raising flour (see page 15 for recipe)

¼ teaspoon bicarbonate of soda (baking soda), sifted

½ cup (100 g/3½ oz) brown sugar

½ teaspoon ground cinnamon

1 large ripe pear, grated, plus a few slices to decorate

½ cup (75 g/2¾ oz) dark chocolate, broken into smaller pieces, plus extra to decorate

⅓ cup (45 g/1½ oz) walnut pieces, plus extra to decorate

Preheat the oven to 190°C/375°F (170°C/325°F fan-forced) with the oven rack positioned in the middle of the oven.

Line a large 6-hole muffin tin with high-sided muffin wraps (or grease the tin with a little butter or oil if not using papers).

Mix the chia seeds and boiling water together in a small bowl. Set aside for 2–3 minutes to form a gel.

Whisk the eggs, oil and milk together in a separate bowl. Tip in the chia gel and whisk again to break up the gel. Set aside.

Add the dry ingredients to a large bowl and whisk well to combine.

Using a spatula, tip the wet mix into the dry mix and gently fold it through until just mixed. (The mix should still be lumpy.) Fold in the pear, chocolate and walnuts.

Using a ¼ cup spring-loaded ice-cream scoop, take a flat scoop of mixture and empty it into a muffin tin. Repeat the process so you have two scoops per muffin wrap. (The mixture should be about two-thirds of the way up each muffin wrap, leaving room for the muffins to rise.)

Decorate the top of each muffin with a couple of slices of pear, some chocolate chunks and a few walnut pieces, transfer to the oven and bake for approximately 20 minutes, then rotate the tray and continue to bake for a further 10 minutes, or until the muffins are lightly golden and a skewer inserted into the centre of each comes out clean.

Remove the muffins from the oven and leave to cool in the tin for 10 minutes before turning out onto a wire rack. Serve warm or at room temperature.

STORAGE

These muffins will keep stored in an airtight container in the refrigerator for up to 3 days, or in the freezer for up to 1 month.

TIPS

- Be sure to use ripe pears, as they make the muffin moister and sweeter. Grating the pear means that it will be better dispersed throughout the mix. If it goes brown while you are preparing the muffins, don't worry; the end result will still be the same.
- I like to use dark chocolate here (and in most of my baking) as it's more intense and less sweet than regular chocolate. Chunks of chocolate as opposed to chips make the muffins look more rustic, but feel free to use the latter instead if that's what you have to hand.

Peach and Basil Muffins

MAKES 6 LARGE MUFFINS

Peach and basil, together? Absolutely! The basil gives the peaches a fabulously earthy flavour that transports me to the Mediterranean. Use the sweetest, juiciest peaches you can lay your hands on for the moistest muffins.

1 tablespoon chia seeds

¼ cup (60 ml/2 fl oz) boiling water

2 eggs

½ cup (125 ml/4 fl oz) light oil (e.g. sunflower, rice bran, canola, light olive oil) or melted butter

1 cup (250 ml/9 fl oz) milk (or non-dairy alternative)

1⅔ cups (275 g/9¾ oz) gluten-free self-raising flour (see page 15 for recipe)

¼ teaspoon bicarbonate of soda (baking soda), sifted

½ cup (100 g/3½ oz) brown sugar

½ teaspoon ground cinnamon

1¼ cups (200 g/7 oz) finely chopped fresh ripe peaches, plus slices to decorate

10 large fresh basil leaves, finely shredded, plus extra to decorate

raw sugar, to decorate

Preheat the oven to 190°C/375°F (170°C/325°F fan-forced) with the oven rack positioned in the middle of the oven.

Line a large 6-hole muffin tin with high-sided muffin wraps (or grease the tin with a little butter or oil if not using papers).

Mix the chia seeds and boiling water together in a small bowl. Set aside for 2–3 minutes to form a gel.

Whisk the eggs, oil and milk together in a separate bowl. Tip in the chia gel and whisk again to break up the gel. Set aside.

Add the dry ingredients to a large bowl and whisk well to combine.

Using a spatula, tip the wet mix into the dry mix and gently fold it through until just mixed. (The mix should still be lumpy.) Fold in the chopped peaches and basil.

Using a ¼ cup spring-loaded ice-cream scoop, take a flat scoop of mixture and empty it into a muffin wrap. Repeat the process so you have two scoops per muffin wrap. (The mix should be about two-thirds of the way up each muffin wrap, leaving enough room for the muffins to rise.)

Decorate the top of each muffin with a couple of slices of peach, a few shredded basil leaves and a light sprinkling of raw sugar, transfer to the oven and bake for approximately 20 minutes, then rotate the tray and continue to bake for a further 10 minutes, until the muffins are lightly golden and a skewer inserted into the centre of each comes out clean.

Remove the muffins from the oven and leave to cool in the tin for 10 minutes before turning out onto a wire rack. Serve warm or at room temperature.

STORAGE

These muffins will keep stored in an airtight container in the refrigerator for up to 3 days, or in the freezer for up to 1 month.

TIPS

- The raw sugar sprinkled on top helps to caramelise the peach and create a slight crunch.
- This recipe does not work with dried basil, as it's too pungent (fresh basil is fragrant, so it complements the peaches well). To shred the basil, pull the leaves off the stems and pile them on top of one another. Shred the leaves with a sharp knife, making sure not to bruise them, so they stay green, rather than turn black.

Mango, Lime and Coconut Muffins (page 34), Peach and Basil Muffins (page 31), Pear, Dark Chocolate and Walnut Muffins (page 30)

Mango, Lime and Coconut Muffins

MAKES 6 LARGE MUFFINS

If summer was a muffin, it would be this one. Each of the three hero ingredients is amazing in its own right, but together they are extraordinary.

1 tablespoon chia seeds

¼ cup (60 ml/2 fl oz) boiling water

2 eggs

½ cup (125 ml/4 fl oz) light oil (e.g. sunflower, rice bran, canola, light olive oil) or melted butter

1 cup (250 ml/9 fl oz) milk (or non-dairy alternative)

1⅔ cups (275 g/9¾ oz) gluten-free self-raising flour (see page 15 for recipe)

¼ teaspoon bicarbonate of soda (baking soda), sifted

½ cup (100 g/3½ oz) brown sugar

½ teaspoon ground cinnamon

1¼ cups (200 g/7 oz) finely chopped fresh ripe mango, plus extra to decorate

finely grated zest of 2 limes

½ cup (30 g/1 oz) coconut flakes, plus extra to decorate

Preheat the oven to 190°C/375°F (170°C/325°F fan-forced) with the oven rack positioned in the middle of the oven.

Line a large 6-hole muffin tin with high-sided muffin wraps (or grease the tin with a little butter or oil if not using papers).

Mix the chia seeds and boiling water together in a small bowl. Set aside for 2–3 minutes to form a gel.

Whisk the eggs, oil and milk together in a separate bowl. Tip in the chia gel and whisk again to break up the gel. Set aside.

Add the dry ingredients to a large bowl and whisk well to combine.

Using a spatula, tip the wet mix into the dry mix and gently fold it through until just mixed. (The mix should still be lumpy.) Fold in the chopped mango, lime zest and coconut flakes.

Using a ¼ cup spring-loaded ice-cream scoop, take a flat scoop of mixture and empty it into a muffin wrap. Repeat the process so you have two scoops per muffin wrap. (The mix should be about two-thirds of the way up each muffin wrap, leaving enough room for the muffins to rise.)

Decorate the top of each muffin with a few pieces of mango and a light sprinkling of coconut flakes, transfer to the oven and bake for approximately 20 minutes, then rotate the tray and continue to bake for a further 10 minutes, or until the muffins are lightly golden and a skewer inserted into the centre of each comes out clean.

Remove the muffins from the oven and leave to cool in the tin for 10 minutes before turning out onto a wire rack. Serve warm or at room temperature.

STORAGE

These muffins will keep stored in an airtight container in the refrigerator for up to 3 days, or in the freezer for up to 1 month.

TIPS

- Ripe, juicy mangoes lend these muffins extra flavour and sweetness as well as giving the moistest results. My favourite variety to use here is Kensington Pride, which delivers an exceptional flavour.
- Coconut flakes add to the flavour and provide the perfect texture and crunch to the topping. You can substitute shredded coconut if you like, but I think the coconut chips look better. Desiccated coconut, on the other hand, will change the texture of the muffins quite a bit – the mix will be drier, and the end result will be a little on the heavy side.

Nectarine, Orange and Thyme Muffins

MAKES 6 LARGE MUFFINS

I adore fresh fruit with fresh herbs, and they work just as well in a muffin. But a word of caution: fresh thyme has a lovely fragrant, floral flavour but dried thyme is too pungent. And only use ripe, juicy nectarines if you're keen on a moist muffin.

1 tablespoon chia seeds

¼ cup (60 ml/2 fl oz) boiling water

2 eggs

½ cup (125 ml/4 fl oz) light oil (e.g. sunflower, rice bran, canola, light olive oil) or melted butter

1 cup (250 ml/9 fl oz) milk (or non-dairy alternative)

juice and finely grated zest of 1 orange

1⅔ cups (275 g/9¾ oz) gluten-free self-raising flour (see page 15 for recipe)

¼ teaspoon bicarbonate of soda (baking soda), sifted

½ cup (100 g/3½ oz) brown sugar

½ teaspoon ground cinnamon

1¼ cups (200 g/7 oz) finely chopped fresh ripe nectarines, plus extra nectarine slices to decorate

¼ bunch fresh thyme leaves, plus extra leaves to decorate

raw sugar, to decorate

Preheat the oven to 190°C/375°F (170°C/325°F fan-forced) with the oven rack positioned in the middle of the oven.

Line a large 6-hole muffin tin with high-sided muffin wraps (or grease the tin with a little butter or oil if not using papers).

Mix the chia seeds and boiling water together in a small bowl. Set aside for 2–3 minutes to form a gel.

Whisk the eggs, oil, milk and orange juice together in a separate bowl. Tip in the chia gel and whisk again to break up the gel. Set aside.

Add the dry ingredients to a large bowl and whisk well to combine.

Using a spatula, tip the wet mix into the dry mix and gently fold it through until just mixed. (The mix should still be lumpy.) Fold in the nectarines, orange zest and thyme.

Using a ¼ cup spring-loaded ice-cream scoop, take a flat scoop of mixture and empty it into a muffin wrap. Repeat the process so you have two scoops per muffin wrap. (The mix should be about two-thirds of the way up each muffin wrap, leaving enough room for the muffins to rise.)

Decorate the top of each muffin with a couple of slices of nectarine, a few thyme leaves and a sprinkle of raw sugar, transfer to the oven and bake for approximately 20 minutes, then rotate the tray and continue to bake for a further 10 minutes, or until the muffins are lightly golden and a skewer inserted into the centre of each comes out clean.

Remove the muffins from the oven and leave to cool in the tin for 10 minutes before turning out onto a wire rack. Serve warm or at room temperature.

STORAGE
These muffins will keep stored in an airtight container in the refrigerator for up to 3 days, or in the freezer for up to 1 month.

TIPS
- The finer the orange zest, the better it will disperse through the muffin mix, giving you a lovely hint of orange rather than the bitterness found in a chunk of rind.
- The raw sugar sprinkled on top helps to caramelise the nectarine and create a slight crunch.

Dark Chocolate, Zucchini and Hazelnut Muffins

MAKES 6 LARGE MUFFINS

Can we just talk about zucchini (courgette) for a moment? It's an unsung hero in my opinion because it's just so versatile. In this recipe its role is just to add moistness, because it has zero flavour when combined with the chocolate and hazelnuts. Once the muffin is cooked you won't see the zucchini at all – ideal if you're trying to get extra veggies into the kids!

1 tablespoon chia seeds

¼ cup (60 ml/2 fl oz) boiling water

2 eggs

½ cup (125 ml/4 fl oz) light oil (e.g. sunflower, rice bran, canola, light olive oil) or melted butter

1 cup (250 ml/9 fl oz) milk (or non-dairy alternative)

1⅓ cups (210 g/7½ oz) gluten-free self-raising flour (see page 15 for recipe)

¼ teaspoon bicarbonate of soda (baking soda), sifted

⅓ cup (40 g/1½ oz) cocoa powder

⅔ cup (125 g/4½ oz) brown sugar

1 teaspoon ground cinnamon

75 g (2¾ oz) dark chocolate, broken into small chunks, plus extra to decorate

½ cup (70 g/2½ oz) finely grated zucchini (courgette)

½ cup (75 g/2¾ oz) hazelnut pieces, plus extra to decorate

Preheat the oven to 190°C/375°F (170°C/325°F fan-forced) with the oven rack positioned in the middle of the oven.

Line a large 6-hole muffin tin with high-sided muffin wraps (or grease the tin with a little butter or oil if not using papers).

Mix the chia seeds and boiling water together in a small bowl. Set aside for 2–3 minutes to form a gel.

Whisk the eggs, oil and milk together in a separate bowl. Tip in the chia gel and whisk again to break up the gel. Set aside.

Add the dry ingredients to a large bowl and whisk well to combine.

Using a spatula, tip the wet mix into the dry mix and gently fold it through until just mixed. (The mix should still be lumpy.) Fold in the chocolate, zucchini and hazelnuts.

Using a ¼ cup spring-loaded ice-cream scoop, take a flat scoop of mixture and empty it into a muffin wrap. Repeat the process so you have two scoops per muffin wrap. (The mix should be about two-thirds of the way up each muffin wrap, leaving enough room for the muffins to rise.)

Decorate the top of each muffin with a few chocolate chunks and hazelnut pieces, transfer to the oven and bake for approximately 20 minutes, then rotate the tray and continue to bake for a further 10 minutes, or until the muffins are lightly golden and a skewer inserted into the centre of each comes out clean.

Remove the muffins from the oven and leave to cool in the tin for 10 minutes before turning out onto a wire rack. Serve warm or at room temperature.

STORAGE
These muffins will keep stored in an airtight container in the refrigerator for up to 3 days, or in the freezer for up to 1 month.

TIPS
- Dairy-free chocolate is now widely available in supermarkets and will work in this recipe.
- While the hazelnuts add the perfect crunch and their flavour works perfectly with the dark chocolate, walnuts or pecans would work very well too.

CUPCAKES, SLICES and SCONES

I like to think of the recipes in this chapter as the essentials that everyone needs to know. They're simple and quick to make and bake (once you've mastered the basics), and if you have these in your gluten-free repertoire you're off to a flying start.

38–57

Vanilla Cupcakes with Vanilla Buttercream

MAKES 12 CUPCAKES

Gluten-free cupcakes aren't exactly child's play to make. After much experimentation, I've worked out the non-negotiables: never overmix the batter and always cook at a lower temperature. If you follow these rules, you'll end up with delightfully light and spongy results.

1¾ cups (290 g/10¼ oz) gluten-free self-raising flour (see page 15 for recipe)

145 g (5 oz) unsalted butter (or non-dairy alternative), cut into small cubes and at room temperature

¾ cup (165 g/5¾ oz) caster (superfine) sugar

3 eggs, at room temperature

¼ cup (60 ml/2 fl oz) light oil (e.g. sunflower, rice bran, canola, light olive oil)

1 teaspoon vanilla bean paste or 1 vanilla pod, split lengthways and seeds scraped

⅓ cup (80 ml/2½ fl oz) milk (or non-dairy alternative)

VANILLA BUTTERCREAM

115 g (4 oz) unsalted butter (or non-dairy alternative), cut into small cubes and at room temperature

1½ cups (185 g/6½ oz) gluten-free icing (confectioners') sugar, sifted

1 egg white

1 teaspoon lemon juice

1 teaspoon vanilla bean paste or 1 vanilla pod, split lengthways and seeds scraped

Preheat the oven to 160°C/315°F (150°C/300°F fan-forced) with the oven rack positioned in the middle of the oven.

Line a 12-hole cupcake pan with paper cases.

Sift the flour into a large bowl. Set aside.

Cream the butter and sugar together in the bowl of a stand mixer with the paddle attachment fitted, or in a mixing bowl with a hand mixer, until pale and fluffy.

Reduce the speed to low–medium and add the eggs one at a time, mixing well after each addition, then add the oil and vanilla and mix until well combined. Turn off the mixer, add half of the flour and baking powder mix together with half the milk and gently fold in. Repeat with the remaining flour mix and milk, being careful not to overmix.

Using a ¼ cup spring-loaded ice-cream scoop, take a slightly heaped scoop (approx. 60 g/2 oz) of mixture and empty it into one of the paper cases so that it is half full. Repeat with the rest of the mixture, being sure not to overfill the cases, as the mixture will double in size on cooking.

Bake for approximately 20 minutes, rotating three-quarters of the way through cooking, or until the cupcakes are very lightly coloured and firm to the touch.

Remove the cupcakes from the oven, transfer the tin to a wire rack and leave to cool completely.

While the cupcakes are cooking, make the buttercream. Add the butter and icing sugar to the bowl of a stand mixer and cream together until pale, then add the egg white, lemon juice and vanilla. Mix on medium–high speed for 2 minutes to combine. (Alternatively, mix the ingredients together in a mixing bowl with a hand mixer.)

Once cool, ice the cupcakes with the buttercream as you wish. Enjoy.

TIPS
- The softer the butter, the quicker your butter and sugar will become pale and creamy, so be careful not to over-cream the mix! This is especially the case when using non-dairy butter.
- Using fresh vanilla or vanilla paste will not only enhance the flavour but also give you lovely flecks of vanilla seeds through your batter.

STORAGE

The un-iced cupcakes will stay fresh in an airtight container at room temperature for 2 days. The buttercream will keep up to 1 week when refrigerated. To use, simply let the buttercream come to room temperature and remix either by hand or with a mixer for 1 minute.

Lemon Cupcakes with Lemon Glaze

MAKES 12 CUPCAKES

If you're a lover of lemons as I am, this recipe is for you. It's just so deliciously fresh and zesty.

1¾ cups (290 g/10¼ oz) gluten-free self-raising flour (see page 15 for recipe)

¼ cup (60 ml/2 fl oz) milk (or non-dairy alternative)

juice and finely grated zest of 1 lemon

145 g (5 oz) unsalted butter (or non-dairy alternative), cut into small cubes and at room temperature

¾ cup (165 g/5¾ oz) caster (superfine) sugar

3 eggs, at room temperature

¼ cup (60 ml/2 fl oz) light oil (e.g. sunflower, rice bran, canola, light olive oil)

LEMON GLAZE

2 cups (250 g/9 oz) gluten-free icing (confectioners') sugar, sifted

juice and finely grated zest of 1 lemon, plus strands of extra zest to decorate

STORAGE

These cupcakes will stay fresh in an airtight container at room temperature for 2 days.

Preheat the oven to 160°C/315°F (150°C/300°F fan-forced) with the oven rack positioned in the middle of the oven.

Line a 12-hole cupcake pan with paper cases.

Sift the flour a into a large bowl. Set aside.

Mix the milk and lemon juice together in a small bowl. Set aside.

Add the butter and sugar to the bowl of a stand mixer with the paddle attachment fitted and cream together, starting at a low speed and gradually increasing speed to medium, until pale and fluffy. (Alternatively, mix the ingredients together in a mixing bowl with a hand mixer.)

Reduce the speed to low–medium and add the eggs one at a time, mixing well after each addition. Add the oil and lemon zest and mix until well combined. Turn off the mixer, add half the flour and half the milk mixture and gently fold in. Repeat with the remaining flour and milk mixture, being careful not to overmix.

Using a ¼ spring-loaded ice-cream scoop, take a slightly heaped scoop (approx. 60 g/2 oz) of mixture and empty it into a paper case so that it is half full. Repeat with the rest of the mixture and paper cases, being sure not to overfill the cases, as the mixture will double in size on cooking.

Bake for 20–25 minutes, rotating three-quarters of the way through cooking, or until the cupcakes are very lightly coloured and firm to the touch.

Remove the cupcakes from the oven, transfer the tin to a wire rack and leave to cool completely.

Meanwhile, make the glaze. In a small mixing bowl, mix the icing sugar, lemon juice and zest together until smooth.

Take a cupcake and dip the top into the glaze, then turn it over, sprinkle with lemon zest and leave to set. Repeat with the remaining cupcakes.

TIPS
- Baking the cupcakes at a lower temperature ensures a slow even rise without too much colour, perfect for a cupcake.
- To keep the lemon zest decoration fresh longer, simply dip it into some sugar syrup to coat the strands and squeeze out any excess syrup. For a thicker/thinner glaze, add a little more icing sugar or lemon juice as preferred.

STORAGE
The un-iced cupcakes will stay fresh in an airtight container at room temperature for 2 days. The ganache will keep up to 1 week when refrigerated. To use, simply let the ganache come to room temperature and remix by hand.

Dark Chocolate Cupcakes with Chocolate Ganache

MAKES 12 CUPCAKES

Decadent, rich, utterly delicious – think of this as the ultimate adult cupcake.

1½ cups (250 g/9 oz) gluten-free self-raising flour (see page 15 for recipe)

⅓ cup (40 g/1½ oz) cocoa powder, sifted

145 g (5 oz) unsalted butter (or non-dairy alternative), cut into small cubes and at room temperature

1 cup (220 g/7¾ oz) caster (superfine) sugar

3 eggs, at room temperature

¼ cup (60 ml/2 fl oz) light oil (e.g. sunflower, rice bran, canola, light olive oil)

1 teaspoon vanilla bean extract

100 g (3½ oz) dark chocolate, roughly chopped

⅓ cup (80 ml/2½ fl oz) milk (or non-dairy alternative)

CHOCOLATE GANACHE

200 ml (7 fl oz) single (pure) cream (or non-dairy alternative)

200 g (7 oz) dark chocolate, broken into small pieces, plus extra shavings to decorate

40 g (1½ oz) unsalted butter (or non-dairy alternative), cut into small cubes and at room temperature

Preheat the oven to 170°C/325°F (150°C/300°F fan-forced) with the oven rack positioned in the middle of the oven.

Line a 12-hole cupcake pan with paper cases.

Sift the flour and cocoa into a bowl and whisk to combine. Set aside.

Add the butter and sugar to the bowl of a stand mixer with the paddle attachment fitted and cream together, starting on low speed and gradually increasing to medium, until pale and fluffy. (Alternatively, mix the ingredients together in a mixing bowl with a hand mixer.)

Reduce the mixing speed to low–medium and add the eggs one at a time, mixing well after each addition, then add the oil and vanilla and continue to mix until well combined. Turn off the mixer, add the chocolate, half the flour mixture and half the milk and gently fold in. Repeat with the remaining flour mixture and milk, being careful not to overmix.

Using a ¼ cup spring-loaded ice-cream scoop, take a heaped scoop (approx. 65 g/2¼ oz) of mixture and empty it into one of the paper cases so that it is two-thirds full. Repeat with the rest of the mixture and paper cases, being sure not to overfill the cases, as the mixture will double in size on cooking.

Bake for approximately 20 minutes, rotating three-quarters of the way through cooking, or until the cupcakes are very lightly coloured and firm to the touch.

Remove the cupcakes from the oven, transfer the tin to a wire rack and leave to cool completely.

When the cupcakes are cool, make the ganache. Bring the cream just to the boil, remove from the heat, add the chocolate and stir until melted. Add the butter and stir until nice and smooth.

Take a cupcake and dip the top of it into the ganache mixture, then turn it over, sprinkle with chocolate shavings and leave to set.

TIP
- For a thicker ganache, make the mixture as above, then lightly whisk until it cools slightly and thickens (be careful not to overmix it or you won't be able to work with it). Apply the thicker ganache to the cupcake with a small cake spatula or butter knife, or pipe on top. Then top with chocolate shavings as before.

Lamingtons

MAKES 6 LAMINGTONS

It's un-Australian not to be able to enjoy this iconic Australian cake! My recipe is both gluten- and dairy-free and will give you a beautifully light result that will make everyone feel included.

⅓ cup (115 g/4 oz) good raspberry jam

300 g (10½ oz) cocoa, sifted

100 g (3½ oz) gluten-free icing (confectioners') sugar, sifted

⅓ cup (80 ml/2½ fl oz) coconut oil

300 ml (10½ fl oz) boiling water

3 cups (195 g/7 oz) shredded coconut

SPONGE

7 large eggs

¾ cup (165 g/5¾ oz) caster (superfine) sugar

⅔ cup (110 g/3¾ oz) gluten-free self-raising flour (see page 15 for recipe)

STORAGE

The finished lamingtons can be stored in the freezer for up to 1 week. Remove from the freezer and leave to sit for 20 minutes before serving.

Preheat the oven to 180°C/350°F (160°C/315°F fan-forced) with the oven rack positioned in the middle of the oven. Grease a 32 x 18 x 3 cm (13 x 7 x 1¼ in) baking tin and line the base with baking paper.

For the sponge, whisk together the eggs and sugar in a saucepan set over a medium heat. Once the mix is hot to the touch (around 65°C/150°F), transfer it to the bowl of a stand mixer with the whisk attachment and whisk on high speed for 7–8 minutes, until light, creamy and doubled in volume.

Remove the bowl from the mixer and gradually sift in the flour, folding it through gently with a spatula as you go. Continue until all the flour has been added and everything is completely combined, then spoon the batter evenly into the prepared tin and bake for 30–35 minutes, until golden and lightly firm to the touch. Remove from the oven and leave to cool completely.

Once cool, turn the sponge out onto a chopping board. Peel the baking paper off the base of the sponge and cut the cake in half horizontally using a bread knife.

Warm the jam a little and spread it generously over one of the sponge halves, then stack the other half of the sponge on top and even up the sides with your knife.

Cut the sponge sandwich into portion-sized pieces and arrange these on a plate or a wire rack. Transfer the plate or rack to the freezer and leave the sponge for 30 minutes to harden (this will make it easier to handle for icing).

Whisk together the cocoa, icing sugar, coconut oil and boiling water in a large mixing bowl until smooth and free of lumps.

Remove the sponge from the freezer and dip each portion into the chocolate icing, making sure it's completely coated on all sides. Sprinkle all over with shredded coconut, then transfer to a lined baking tray for the coating to set.

The lamingtons are best left to set in the freezer for at least 15 minutes before serving.

TIPS
- Be sure to freeze the sponge slightly before dipping it into the icing – if the sponge is too soft it can fall apart in the icing mix.
- Replace the raspberry jam with strawberry jam if you prefer.

Decadent Dark Chocolate Brownies

MAKES 10 BROWNIES

Some people consider anything dairy-free to be somehow inferior, but this is not the case here. Coconut oil gives these brownies a wonderful edge that others just don't have. Yes, you can use butter instead, but do try the coconut route at least once – combined with the coffee (which lends the brownies depth of flavour rather than an obvious coffee taste) it results in brownies that really are something else.

1 cup (250 ml/9 fl oz) coconut oil or other light oil (e.g. sunflower, rice bran, canola, light olive oil) or melted butter

2 cups (340 g/11½ oz) dark chocolate chips (or finely chopped dairy-free chocolate)

1½ cups (250 g/9 oz) gluten-free plain (all-purpose) flour (see page 15 for recipe)

½ cup (55 g/2 oz) cocoa, sifted

½ teaspoon salt

1 teaspoon ground espresso-style coffee (optional)

6 large eggs, at room temperature

1 teaspoon vanilla extract

1 cup (185 g/6½ oz) brown sugar

1 cup (220 g/7¾ oz) white sugar or raw sugar

STORAGE

Brownies will keep in an airtight container in the fridge for up to 5 days or in the freezer for up to 1 month.

Preheat the oven to 180°C/350°F (160°C/315°F fan-forced) with the oven rack positioned in the middle of the oven.

Grease a 32 x 18 x 3 cm (13 x 7 x 1¼ in) brownie tray and line the sides with baking paper.

Melt the coconut oil and half the chocolate chips together in a small saucepan over low heat or in a bowl in the microwave for 1 minute, or until the chocolate is half melted. Stir until completely melted and set aside to cool slightly.

Whisk together the flour, cocoa, salt and ground coffee, if using, in a large bowl.

Whisk the eggs, vanilla and sugars together in a separate bowl.

Add the melted chocolate and oil to the wet mix and whisk until just combined (do not overmix).

Using a spatula, tip the wet mix into the dry mix and gently fold it through until everything is just mixed together and the flour is completely incorporated. Fold in the remaining chocolate chips.

Tip the mix into the lined brownie tray, then transfer to the oven and bake for 40–45 minutes, rotating the tin halfway through for even cooking, until the top feels firm when pressed gently but a skewer inserted into the centre comes out with a little chocolate mix still clinging to it.

Once cooked, remove from the oven and leave to sit in the tin on a wire rack to cool for 15 minutes. Slice and enjoy warm (using a sharp knife heated under running hot water so it slices the brownie neatly without sticking) or leave to cool completely before cutting and serving.

TIPS

- Be very careful not to burn the chocolate when melting. (There really is no coming back from that – you simply have to start again.) Also, be careful not to overcook the brownies, particularly if you like them a little soft and gooey.
- The chocolate chips folded in at the end can be replaced with walnuts, pecans or coconut flakes.

Raspberry and Coconut Slice

MAKES 10 SLICES

Slices are so nostalgic to me, bringing back memories of my childhood. This is one of my favourites, contrasting the sweetness of coconut and an Anzac biscuit base with the tartness of raspberries.

1 batch of uncooked Anzac Biscuit dough (see page 60)

3½ cups (430 g/15¼ oz) fresh or frozen raspberries

¼ cup (60 ml/2 fl oz) coconut oil, melted

2 tablespoons golden syrup

2 cups (130 g/4½ oz) shredded coconut

STORAGE

Slices will keep in an airtight container in the fridge for up to 1 week or in the freezer for up to 1 month (allow it to come to room temperature before serving).

Preheat the oven to 160°C/315°F (140°C/275°F fan-forced) with the oven rack positioned in the middle of the oven.

Grease a 32 x 18 x 3 cm (13 x 7 x 1¼ in) brownie tray and line with baking paper.

Press the uncooked Anzac biscuit dough evenly over the base, then arrange the raspberries over the biscuit dough in an even layer and press lightly with a fork.

In a bowl, whisk together the coconut oil and golden syrup, then fold in the shredded coconut until the coconut is completely coated. Tip the mix out over the raspberries and level out gently with the back of a spoon.

Bake for 25–30 minutes, rotating halfway through for even cooking, until golden.

Remove from the oven and leave to cool. Once cool, slice and enjoy.

TIPS

- I use golden syrup to coat the coconut as that's what I use in my Anzac biscuits, though you can always replace this with rice syrup, coconut syrup or agave syrup instead if you like. If the coconut on top starts to brown early in the baking, cover loosely with aluminium foil and continue to bake until the Anzac base is golden and cooked through.
- The raspberries can be replaced with any other berry. Have a look and choose what's in season and looking good.

Buttermilk Scones

MAKES 6 LARGE SCONES

There's nowhere to hide with plain scones. If the texture isn't right, there's not much you can do to redeem them. But if you follow my recipe closely and heed my tips, you'll end up with an impressive batch of beautifully light and fluffy, well-risen scones. The dairy-free version of this recipe works really well too!

2 cups (330 g/11½ oz) gluten-free self-raising flour (see page 15 for recipe), plus extra for dusting

1 teaspoon gluten-free baking powder

1½ teaspoons xanthan gum

¾ teaspoon bicarbonate of soda (baking soda)

60 g (2¼ oz) cold unsalted butter (or non-dairy alternative), cut into small cubes

¼ teaspoon salt

⅓ cup (75 g/2¾ oz) caster (superfine) sugar

1 egg, at room temperature

1 cup (250 ml/9 fl oz) buttermilk (or 200 ml/7 fl oz non-dairy alternative mixed with 2 tablespoons lemon juice)

Preheat the oven to 170°C/325°F (150°C/300°F fan-forced) with the oven rack positioned in the middle of the oven.

Line a baking tray with baking paper.

Sift the flour, baking powder, xanthan gum and bicarbonate of soda into a large bowl. Whisk to combine.

Rub in the butter using your fingers until the mixture resembles fine breadcrumbs. (It should not be lumpy – if it is, keep rubbing until there are no lumps.) Stir in the salt and sugar with a dessert spoon.

Add the egg and stir to combine, then gently stir in half the buttermilk until just mixed in. Stir in the remaining buttermilk to form a moist dough.

Turn the dough onto a lightly floured surface and knead very gently to form a disc approximately 4 cm (1½ in) thick. Lightly flour the top of the dough.

Dip a 6 cm (2½ in) circular cutter in flour, then use it to cut out your scones – bringing the dough back together, re-flouring it and flattening it to get it back to the desired thickness as necessary. Transfer the scones to the prepared baking tray, spacing them evenly.

Bake for 20–25 minutes, rotating the tray halfway through for even cooking, until lightly golden brown on top. Remove from the oven and leave to cool slightly. Serve warm with your favourite sweet toppings.

STORAGE

These scones will keep stored in an airtight container for up to 3 days, or in the freezer for up to 1 month.

TIPS

- Sifting the dry ingredients together like this ensures there are no lumps and helps to create the lightness you need for scones.
- It's really important when making scones that you don't overmix the dough, otherwise they will be heavy and dense. Likewise, kneading scone dough is a very quick process – it's important not to overwork it. The less you touch the dough, the better!

Date, Honey and Thyme Scones

MAKES 7 LARGE SCONES

If you can't find fresh dates, you can always use dried ones – soaked in boiling water then drained and dried – here instead. However, please don't use dried thyme, as it will overwhelm the flavour. Fresh thyme, which is wonderfully fragrant and floral, is the definite go-to here.

2 cups (330 g/11½ oz) gluten-free self-raising flour (see page 15 for recipe), plus extra for dusting

1 teaspoon gluten-free baking powder

1½ teaspoons xanthan gum

¾ teaspoon bicarbonate of soda (baking soda)

60 g (2¼ oz) cold unsalted butter, cut into small cubes (or non-dairy alternative), plus extra to serve

¼ teaspoon salt

1 egg, at room temperature

¼ cup (60 ml/2 fl oz) runny honey, plus extra to serve

¾ cup (185 ml/6 fl oz) buttermilk (or 140 ml/4½ fl oz non-dairy alternative mixed with 1½ tablespoons lemon juice)

1½ cups (240 g/8½ oz) fresh dates, seeded and chopped small

2 tablespoons fresh thyme leaves

Preheat the oven to 170°C/325°F (150°C/300°F fan-forced) with the oven rack positioned in the middle of the oven.

Line a baking tray with baking paper.

Sift the flour, baking powder, xanthan gum and bicarbonate of soda into a large bowl. Whisk to combine.

Rub in the butter using your fingers until the mixture resembles fine breadcrumbs. (It should not be lumpy – if it is, keep rubbing until there are no lumps.) Stir in the salt with a dessert spoon.

Add the egg and honey and stir to combine, then gently stir in half of the buttermilk until just mixed in. Add the dates and thyme, then stir in the remaining buttermilk to form a moist dough.

Turn the dough onto a lightly floured surface and knead very gently to form a disc approximately 4 cm (1½ in) thick. Lightly flour the top of the dough.

Dip a 6 cm (2½ in) circular cutter in flour, then use it to cut out your scones – bringing the dough back together, re-flouring it and flattening it to get it back to the desired thickness as necessary. Transfer the scones to the lined baking tray, spacing them evenly.

Bake for 25–30 minutes, rotating the tray halfway through for even cooking, until lightly golden brown on top. Remove from the oven and leave to cool slightly. Serve warm with butter and a little more honey.

TIPS
- Using cold butter will make it easier to rub it into the flour without it sticking to your fingers. A non-dairy alternative will be softer and a little trickier to work with, but the end result will be the same.
- Dusting the top of the scone dough with a little flour will make cutting easier, while dusting the cutter between scones will help prevent the dough from sticking to it.

STORAGE
These scones will keep stored in an airtight container for up to 3 days, or in the freezer for up to 1 month.

Blueberry and Lemon Scones

MAKES 7 LARGE SCONES

As always, a gentle touch is the secret to a great scone. Gently stir, gently fold, gently knead and you'll be right. This particular recipe – with the freshness of lemon and sweetness of berries – is a real winner.

2 cups (330 g/11½ oz) gluten-free self-raising flour (see page 15 for recipe), plus extra for dusting

1 teaspoon gluten-free baking powder

1½ teaspoons xanthan gum

¾ teaspoon bicarbonate of soda (baking soda)

60 g (2¼ oz) cold unsalted butter, cut into small cubes (or non-dairy alternative)

¼ teaspoon salt

⅓ cup (75 g/2¾ oz) caster (superfine) sugar

1 egg, at room temperature

1 cup (250 ml/9 fl oz) buttermilk (or 200 ml/7 fl oz non-dairy alternative mixed with 2 tablespoons lemon juice)

1 cup (155 g/5½ oz) fresh or frozen blueberries

finely grated zest of 1 large lemon

Preheat the oven to 170°C/325°F (150°C/300°F fan-forced) with the oven rack positioned in the middle of the oven.

Line a baking tray with baking paper.

Sift the flour, baking powder, xanthan gum and bicarbonate of soda into a large bowl. Whisk to combine.

Rub in the butter using your fingers until the mixture resembles fine breadcrumbs. (It should not be lumpy – if it is, keep rubbing until there are no lumps.) Stir in the salt and sugar with a dessert spoon.

Add the egg and stir to combine, then gently stir in half the buttermilk until just mixed in. Add the blueberries and lemon zest. Stir in the remaining buttermilk to form a moist dough.

Turn the dough onto a lightly floured surface and knead very gently to form a disc approximately 4 cm (1½ in) thick. Lightly flour the top of the dough.

Dip a 6 cm (2½ in) circular cutter in flour, then use it to cut out your scones – bringing the dough back together, re-flouring it and flattening it to get it back to the desired thickness as necessary. Transfer the scones to the lined baking tray, spacing them evenly.

Bake for 25–30 minutes, rotating the tray halfway through for even cooking, until lightly golden brown on top. Remove from the oven and leave to cool slightly. Serve warm with butter.

TIPS

- Lining the tray with baking paper ensures the scones don't stick and will make them easier to move around, should they need to be moved.
- If you don't have fresh blueberries and want to use frozen instead, be sure to keep them frozen until they need to be added. That way they won't defrost, leak juice and turn the scone batter purple. Just be aware that you might need to add a few minutes to the baking time as the berries will make the dough cold.

STORAGE

These scones will stay fresh in an airtight container for 2 days, or in the freezer for up to 1 month.

Buttermilk Scones (page 53), Date, Honey and Thyme Scones (page 54), Blueberry and Lemon Scones (page 55)

BISCUITS

A pantry essential, biscuits are – sadly – often disappointing
when gluten-free. But not these ones! The following classics
are quick, easy to make and taste incredible.
Try them for yourself and see.

58–69

Anzac Biscuits

MAKES 10 BISCUITS

I judge an Anzac biscuit on the balance of crisp and chew: it needs to be a little crisp on the outside while still nice and chewy on the inside. This recipe achieves this holy grail but if you like yours really crisp, just bake them for a few minutes longer.

⅔ cup (110 g/3¾ oz) gluten-free plain (all-purpose) flour (see page 15 for recipe)

¾ cup (65 g/2¼ oz) desiccated coconut

1 cup (120 g/4¼ oz) quinoa flakes

¼ cup (35 g/1¼ oz) raw sugar

¼ cup (45 g/1½ oz) brown sugar

½ cup (125 ml/4 fl oz) coconut oil

2 tablespoons golden syrup

¾ teaspoon bicarbonate of soda (baking soda)

2 tablespoons boiling water

Preheat the oven to 170°C/325°F (150°C/300°F fan-forced). Line two baking trays with baking paper.

Add the flour, coconut, quinoa and sugars to a bowl and whisk together to combine.

Gently heat the coconut oil and golden syrup in a small saucepan until warm. Mix the bicarbonate of soda and boiling water together in a cup, then add to the saucepan and stir together until frothy. Remove the pan from the heat, tip the wet mix into the bowl with the dry ingredients and mix together well.

Divide the mix into 10 equal-sized pieces (approximately 50 g/1¾ oz each) and roll into balls. Arrange the balls on the prepared trays, spacing them 8 cm (3¼ in) apart to allow room for them to spread while baking. Using a fork, flatten slightly so that the biscuits have a diameter of 5 cm (2 in).

Bake for 18–20 minutes, rotating the trays halfway through for even cooking, until a deep golden brown. Remove from the oven and leave the biscuits to cool on the trays. Enjoy.

STORAGE

Raw Anzac dough, portioned into balls and flattened into discs, can be stored in the freezer and cooked at a later time (be sure to separate the discs with baking paper when freezing so they don't stick to each other). To bake from frozen, reduce the oven temperature by 10°C (50°F) and bake for 5 minutes longer. Fresh Anzacs can be stored in an airtight container or jar for up to 1 week.

TIPS
- Like any biscuits, these Anzacs will be softest when just cooked and will harden as they cool down.
- Replacing the raw sugar with extra brown sugar will give you Anzacs that spread thinner while baking.

Gingerbread Biscuits

MAKES ABOUT 30 BISCUITS

I've never met a child who didn't love a gingerbread biscuit, especially one with a fun shape. They can be just as appealing to adults craving a small but tasty sweet treat to enjoy with a cup of tea.

2⅓ cups (385 g/13½ oz) gluten-free plain (all-purpose) flour (see page 15 for recipe)

3 teaspoons xanthan gum

¼ teaspoon bicarbonate of soda (baking soda), sifted

½ teaspoon salt

2 tablespoons ground ginger

1 teaspoon ground cinnamon

1 teaspoon ground nutmeg

160 g (5½ oz) unsalted butter (or non-dairy alternative), cut into small cubes

1 cup (185 g/6½ oz) brown sugar

⅓ cup (80 ml/2½ fl oz) runny honey

3 large egg yolks, at room temperature

1 large egg, beaten

Sift the flour, xanthan gum, bicarbonate of soda, salt and spices into a bowl and whisk together thoroughly. Set aside.

Add the butter, brown sugar and honey to the bowl of a stand mixer with the whisk attachment and cream together until light and fluffy. (Alternatively, mix the ingredients together in a mixing bowl with a hand mixer.)

Slowly add the egg yolks and egg and keep mixing until smooth. Using the paddle attachment, slowly add the sifted dry ingredients to the bowl until everything is just mixed together and the flour is completely incorporated.

Turn the dough onto a baking tray lined with plastic wrap and roughly roll out until the dough is flat. Cover with another layer of plastic wrap, transfer to the refrigerator and leave to rest for 2 hours.

When your dough is ready, preheat the oven to 180°C/350°F (160°C/315°F fan-forced) with the oven rack positioned in the middle of the oven. Line a baking tray with baking paper.

Unwrap the chilled and rested dough and roll it out evenly on a very lightly floured surface to 4 mm (¼ in) thick.

Dip your chosen biscuit cutter into a little flour, then cut out the gingerbread biscuits and place them on the lined tray, spacing them a minimum of 1 cm (½ in) apart. Reroll the dough and repeat the process until all the dough has been used.

Bake for 18–20 minutes, rotating the tray halfway through for even cooking, until lightly golden brown. Remove from the oven and leave on the tray to cool completely.

STORAGE

Gingerbread will stay fresh in an airtight container for 10 days or in the freezer for up to 1 month. The uncooked dough also freezes well for up to 1 month.

TIP

- If the gingerbread biscuits are not crisp enough for your liking once cooled, return them to the oven at the same temperature and bake for another 5–7 minutes.

LIMITED TIME
YUZU ECLAIR
AVAILABLE
EVERY DAY.
YUZU DANISH
AVAILABLE
WEEKEND ONLY

Chocolate Chunk Cookies

MAKES 13–14 COOKIES

A classic cookie if ever there was one. I promised my kids I'd develop a chocolate chip cookie for this book, although I've made the chips more like chunks for maximum gooeyness.

1¼ cups (205 g/7¼ oz) gluten-free plain (all-purpose) flour (see page 15 for recipe)

½ teaspoon xanthan gum

1 teaspoon bicarbonate of soda (baking soda)

150 g (5½ oz) butter, cut into small cubes and at room temperature

⅓ cup (60 g/2¼ oz) brown sugar

⅓ cup (65 g/2¼ oz) raw caster (superfine) sugar

1 teaspoon vanilla extract

1 large egg

250 g/9 oz dark cooking chocolate, broken into small chunks

STORAGE

These biscuits will stay fresh in an airtight container for 7 days. Once rolled into balls, the dough can be frozen for up to 1 month. To bake, simply defrost slightly, flatten and cook as above.

Line three large baking trays with baking paper.

Sift the flour, xanthan gum and bicarbonate of soda into a bowl and whisk together thoroughly.

Add the butter and sugars to the bowl of a stand mixer with the paddle attachment fitted and cream together on low–medium speed for 1 minute. (Alternatively, mix the ingredients together in a mixing bowl with a hand mixer.)

Slowly add the vanilla extract and egg and keep mixing, increasing the speed to medium–high, for 2 minutes, scraping down the sides of the bowl halfway through. Gradually add the sifted dry ingredients until everything is just mixed in. Fold in the chocolate using a spatula, then transfer the bowl to the refrigerator and leave for 20 minutes for the dough to chill and firm.

Divide the chilled dough into 50 g (1¾ oz) portions and shape each into a ball. Arrange the dough balls on the lined trays spread 10 cm (4 in) apart, then transfer to the fridge and leave to chill for 30 minutes. (This will help rest the dough so that when it bakes, it keeps its shape and doesn't spread too far.)

Preheat the oven to 180°C/350°F (160°C/315°F fan-forced) with the oven racks positioned in the middle of the oven. Gently press each dough ball to flatten slightly, then bake the cookies for 12–14 minutes, rotating the trays after 8 minutes, until lightly golden.

Remove from the oven and leave to cool for 5 minutes before transferring to a wire rack to cool completely. These cookies are also delicious eaten warm while the chocolate is gooey.

TIPS
- The dark chocolate can be replaced with any chocolate you prefer.
- To make these into double chocolate cookies, add ¼ cup (30 g/1 oz) cocoa powder to the dry ingredients and decrease the flour quantity by ¼ cup (40 g/1½ oz).

Lemon Shortbread

MAKES APPROXIMATELY 22 BISCUITS

If you're not a citrus fan, you can just leave out the lemon zest and you'll end up with a deliciously buttery plain (and really short) shortbread. But I do love it with a little lemon zing.

1 cup (165 g/5¾ oz) gluten-free plain (all-purpose) flour (see page 15 for recipe)

1 cup (160 g/5½ oz) white rice flour

¾ teaspoon xanthan gum

250 g (9 oz) butter, chopped small and at room temperature

½ cup (110 g/3¾ oz) caster (superfine) sugar

1 teaspoon vanilla extract

½ cup (50 g/1¾ oz) almond meal

zest of 2 lemons

STORAGE

These biscuits will stay fresh in an airtight container for up to 7 days. Uncooked cut-out biscuits can be frozen on the trays for up to 1 month and baked from frozen.

Line 2 large baking trays with baking paper.

Sift the flours and xanthan gum into a bowl and whisk together thoroughly.

Add the butter, sugar and vanilla to the bowl of a stand mixer with the whisk attachment and cream together for 30 seconds. (Alternatively, mix the ingredients together in a mixing bowl with a hand mixer.)

Using the paddle attachment, slowly add the sifted flour mix to the bowl together with the almond meal and lemon zest and mix for 1 minute to form a dough.

Turn the dough out onto a floured surface and knead gently until smooth. Using a rolling pin, gently roll out the dough to 1 cm (½ in) thick. Dip your chosen biscuit cutter into a little flour, then cut out the shortbread and place them on the lined trays, spacing them a minimum of 5–6 cm (2–2½ in) apart. Reroll the dough and repeat the process until all the dough has been used.

Use the tines of a fork to make decorative indents in the shortbread, if you like, then transfer the trays to the refrigerator and leave to rest for 30 minutes. (Resting and chilling the dough will help it to keep its shape and prevent it from spreading too much.)

Preheat the oven to 160°C/315°F (140°C/275°F fan-forced) with the oven racks positioned in the middle of the oven.

Bake the chilled shortbread for 25–30 minutes, rotating the trays halfway through for even cooking, until lightly golden. Remove from the oven and leave to cool for 5 minutes before transferring to a wire rack to cool completely.

TIPS

- You can use any caster sugar in this recipe. (I prefer not to use brown sugar, as it's very moist and can make your biscuit spread really flat.) It's important when making shortbread that you don't over-cream the butter and sugar – the dough is meant to be slightly heavy.
- The xanthan gum helps to prevent the shortbread from spreading out too much while baking. Leaving it out will make your shortbread flatter and a little bit more crumbly.

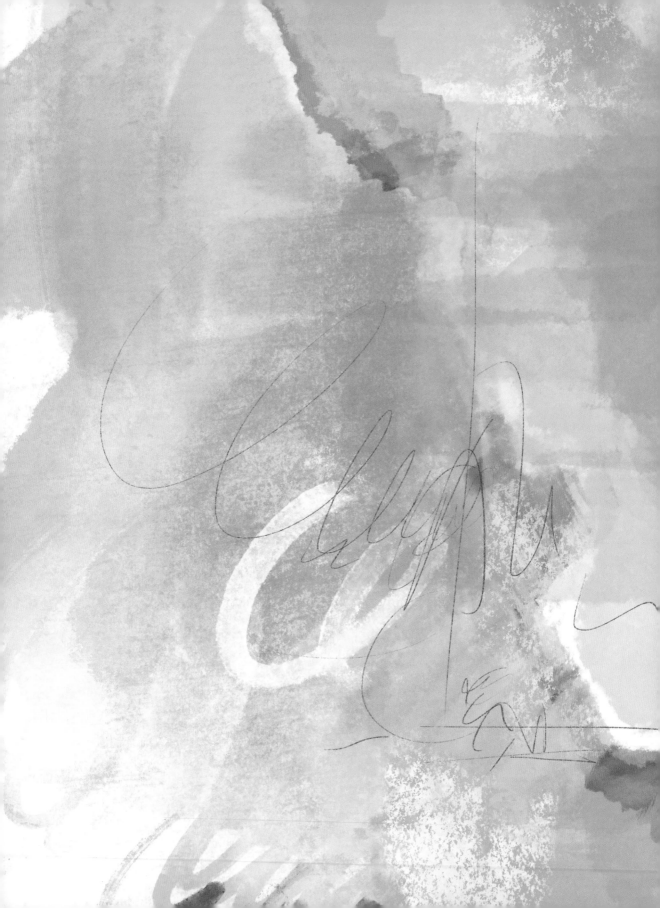

FRUIT CRUMBLES, PANCAKES and CRÊPES

I like to think of the recipes here as weekend-morning
baking treats. Pancakes and crêpes are something of
a weekly staple in our house, while crumbles make an
appearance in winter and are (to my mind, anyway) at their
best as leftovers for breakfast the next morning.

70–81

Fruit Crumble

SERVES 6

I love a warm fruit crumble on a cold day. The recipe here provides a
basic crumble mix and offers up three equally delicious suggestions
for fruit mixes. The addition of flour to the fruit mixes here helps
to make the juices from the fruit thick and syrupy, while adding
shredded coconut and chopped almonds to the crumble mix prevents
it from becoming too flour-heavy and lends it texture and flavour.
While you could use plain (all-purpose) flour for the crumble top,
I like to use self-raising, as it helps it rise and form a great crumb.

CRUMBLE MIX

⅓ cup (55 g/2 oz) gluten-free self-raising flour
(see page 15 for recipe)

⅔ cup (55 g/2 oz) shredded coconut

⅓ cup (55 g/2 oz) almonds, chopped

⅓ cup (60 g/2¼ oz) brown sugar

1 teaspoon ground cinnamon

50 g (1¾ oz) butter, cut into small cubes,
plus extra for greasing

STRAWBERRY, RHUBARB and VANILLA

1 large bunch rhubarb, stalks trimmed
and cut into small bite-sized pieces

1 punnet (250 g/9 oz) fresh strawberries, sliced

finely grated zest and juice of 1 large orange

⅓ cup (60 g/2¼ oz) brown sugar

1 teaspoon ground cinnamon

1 teaspoon vanilla extract

1 tablespoon gluten-free plain (all-purpose)
flour (see page 15 for recipe)

PEAR, BLUEBERRY and CINNAMON

3 large ripe pears, skin on, cored and cut into
small bite-sized pieces

¾ cup (115 g/4 oz) fresh or frozen blueberries

juice of 1 large lemon

⅓ cup (60 g/2¼ oz) brown sugar

1 teaspoon ground cinnamon

1 tablespoon gluten-free plain (all-purpose)
flour (see page 15 for recipe)

APPLE, BOYSENBERRY and LEMON

3 large apples, skin on, cored and cut into
small bite-sized pieces

¾ cup (100 g/3½ oz) fresh or frozen boysenberries

zest and juice of 1 large lemon

⅓ cup (60 g/2¼ oz) brown sugar

1 teaspoon ground cinnamon

1 tablespoon gluten-free plain (all-purpose)
flour (see page 15 for recipe)

Preheat the oven to 170°C/325°F (150°C/300°F fan-forced) with the oven rack positioned in the middle of the oven.

Grease a 17 x 28.5 x 4 cm (6½ x 11¼ x 1½ in) baking dish with a little butter.

Mix all the dry crumble ingredients together in a bowl. Rub in the butter until all mixed in.

Toss your chosen fruit mix into the prepared baking dish and mix together gently.

Scatter the crumble topping over the fruit mix to cover evenly, then transfer to the oven and bake for 50 minutes, or until golden brown. Serve warm with ice cream, cream, Greek yoghurt or thick coconut yoghurt.

STORAGE
Fruit crumble can be stored in the refrigerator for up to 2 days (and is delicious the day after making as a breakfast treat).

TIP
- The butter in the crumble mix can be replaced with non-dairy butter or even coconut oil if you'd prefer (if using coconut oil, 40 g/1½ oz should be plenty). And while I prefer brown sugar as it adds both moisture and a caramel flavour, you can use whatever sugar you like.

Pear, Blueberry and Cinnamon Crumble, Apple, Boysenberry and Lemon Crumble, Strawberry, Rhubarb and Vanilla Crumble (all page 72)

Buttermilk Pancakes

MAKES APPROXIMATELY 8 PANCAKES

These sweet pancakes are fluffy, silky-smooth and mouth-wateringly delicious, thanks largely to a generous amount of butter. They're also just as great using a non-dairy milk alternative with a little lemon juice to make a buttermilk substitute.

¾ cup (125 g/4½ oz) gluten-free self-raising flour (see page 15 for recipe)

¼ teaspoon bicarbonate of soda (baking soda), sifted

1½ tablespoons any granulated sugar or liquid sweetener of choice

1 large egg

350 ml (12 fl oz) buttermilk (or 250 ml/9 fl oz non-dairy milk mixed with 1 tablespoon lemon juice)

25 g (1 oz) unsalted butter (or non-dairy alternative), melted, plus extra for cooking

Sift all the dry ingredients together into a large bowl and whisk to combine.

Whisk the egg and buttermilk together in a separate bowl.

Add the melted butter to the egg mix and whisk again.

Pour the wet mix into the dry mix and whisk until smooth.

Melt a little extra butter in a non-stick frying pan over low–medium heat, tilting the pan to make sure the base is evenly coated.

Using a ladle or serving spoon, drop approximately ⅓ cup (80 ml/ 2½ fl oz) of the batter into the centre of the pan, smoothing it out with the back of your spoon and shaping it into a rough circle approximately 12 cm (4½ in) in diameter.

Cook for 2 minutes, or until bubbles appear on the surface of the pancake and the underside is evenly golden (use your spatula to check), then flip it over and cook for a further 2 minutes, until evenly golden on both sides.

Slide the cooked pancake onto to a plate and transfer to a very low oven to keep warm. Repeat the process until all the pancake mix has been used, adding a little more butter to the pan between pancakes as needed. Serve with your favourite toppings.

STORAGE

Cooked pancakes are best eaten on the day but can be stored in the fridge for up to 1 day and reheated in the pan or microwave when needed.

TIPS

- This pancake batter can be made a day ahead and kept in the fridge. Just whisk before using.
- The addition of sugar doesn't make the pancakes taste too sweet but does allow for them to be enjoyed plain. You can use any sugar you like – a pale sugar will make your pancake lighter in colour, while a darker sugar will do the opposite. If using a liquid sweetener, you may want to slightly reduce the amount of non-dairy milk, if using (they are usually much runnier than ready-made buttermilk, which is thick and creamy).

Banana and Maple Buttermilk Pancakes

MAKES APPROXIMATELY 8 PANCAKES

One of our favourite ways to start the weekend. The bananas in this recipe are caramelised by the maple syrup, producing the yummiest banana caramel flavour. And the pancakes themselves are silky and succulent, thanks to the high butter content. Completely decadent and delicious.

¾ cup (125 g/4½ oz) gluten-free self-raising flour (see page 15 for recipe)

¼ teaspoon bicarbonate of soda (baking soda), sifted

1 tablespoon any granulated sugar or liquid sweetener of choice

1 large egg

350 ml (12 fl oz) buttermilk (or 250 ml/9 fl oz non-dairy milk mixed with 1 tablespoon lemon juice)

80 ml (2½ fl oz) maple syrup, plus extra for serving

25 g (1 oz) unsalted butter (or non-dairy alternative), melted, plus extra for cooking

2 large ripe bananas, peeled

STORAGE

Cooked pancakes are best eaten on the day but can be stored in the fridge for up to 1 day and reheated in the pan or microwave when needed.

Sift all the dry ingredients together into a large bowl and whisk to combine.

Whisk the egg, buttermilk and 2 tablespoons of the maple syrup together in a separate bowl.

Add the melted butter to the egg mix and whisk again.

Pour the wet mix into the dry mix and whisk until smooth.

Cut the two bananas in half lengthways, then slice each half lengthways into 4 pieces (16 pieces in total). Put these to one side.

Melt a little extra butter in a non-stick frying pan over low–medium heat, tilting the pan to make sure the base is evenly coated.

Using a ladle or serving spoon, drop approximately ⅓ cup (80 ml/ 2½ fl oz) of the batter into the centre of the pan, smoothing it out with the back of your spoon and shaping it into a rough circle approximately 12 cm (4½ in) in diameter. Quickly lay two slices of banana over the pancake mix in two lines and gently press them down so they sit flush in the pancake mix.

Cook for 2 minutes, or until bubbles appear on the surface of the pancake and the underside is evenly golden (use your spatula to check). Spoon over 1 teaspoon of maple syrup, then carefully flip it over and cook for a further 2 minutes, until evenly golden on both sides.

Slide the pancake onto a plate with the banana side up and transfer to a very low oven to keep warm. Repeat the process until all the pancake mix and banana slices have been used, adding a little more butter to the pan between pancakes as needed. (For cleaner- looking pancakes, wipe the frying pan out with paper towel after cooking each one.) Serve the pancakes with a little more maple syrup.

TIPS

- The buttermilk is the hero when it comes to helping create light and fluffy pancakes. If you don't have any, simply use milk combined with lemon juice (as milk is thinner than buttermilk, you'll need a little less). Mix the two together and leave to sit for 5 minutes before using. The end result will be similar.
- Using ripe bananas adds more flavour and sweetness as well as better caramelisation, as their sugar content is higher.

Crêpes

MAKES APPROXIMATELY 10 CRÊPES

There are two sorts of people in the world: those who love pancakes and those who love crêpes. I developed this recipe because my eldest daughter, Holly, is the latter, having fallen in love with them at her best friend's house. A sprinkle of lemon and sugar and she's one happy camper.

¾ cup (125 g/4½ oz) gluten-free plain (all-purpose) flour (see page 15 for recipe)

½ teaspoon salt

1 tablespoon any granulated sugar or liquid sweetener of choice

1 large egg

650 ml (22½ fl oz) milk (or non-dairy alternative), plus extra as needed

25 g (1 oz) unsalted butter (or non-dairy alternative), melted, plus extra for cooking

STORAGE

Cooked crêpes are best eaten on the day but can be stored in the fridge for up to 1 day and reheated in the pan or microwave when needed.

Sift the flour into a large bowl. Add the salt and sugar and whisk to combine.

Whisk the egg and milk together in a separate bowl.

Add the melted butter to the egg mix and whisk again.

Pour the wet mix into the dry mix and whisk until smooth. The mix should be runny. Add a splash or two more milk if the batter is still too thick.

Melt a little extra butter in a large non-stick frying pan or crêpe pan approximately 21 cm (8¼ in) in diameter over low heat, tilting the pan to make sure the base is evenly coated.

Using a ladle or serving spoon, drop approximately ⅓ cup (80 ml/2½ fl oz) of batter into the centre of the pan. Lift the pan and tilt to coat the base thinly and evenly.

Cook for 4 minutes, until the underside of the crêpe is evenly golden (use your spatula to check), then flip it over and cook for a further 2 minutes, until evenly golden on both sides.

Slide the cooked crêpe onto a plate and transfer to a very low oven to keep warm. Repeat the process until all the crêpe mix has been used.

Serve with your favourite toppings (ours are lemon juice and sugar).

TIPS

- This crêpe batter can be made a day ahead and kept in the fridge. Just whisk before using.
- The quantity of milk you need can vary depending on the flour blend used. Always start by adding a little less than the full amount, then add more to thin the batter if needed.
- A non-stick crêpe pan is particularly useful as the sides of the pan fan out and are lower than those of a normal frying pan, making it easy to slide the crêpes out of the pan and onto your plate.

LOAVES

I love loaf cakes – portable, versatile, and easy to slice and serve. The recipes that follow are perfect for when you're looking to make a cake that isn't an 'event'. Toasted or iced, they're a great way to enjoy everyday gluten-free baking.

82–91

Banana and Pecan Loaf

MAKES 1 LOAF

The great saviour of overripe bananas. In fact, the more bananas look destined for the compost or the bin, the better they are at making your banana bread deliciously sweet and moist. Chia seeds also help to elevate the result by creating lightness in what could otherwise be an overly dense loaf.

1 tablespoon chia seeds

¼ cup (60 ml/2 fl oz) boiling water

5 large overripe bananas, (about 475 g/1 lb 1 oz peeled bananas), plus 1 banana sliced lengthways

3 large eggs, at room temperature

½ cup (125 ml/4 fl oz) light oil (e.g. sunflower, rice bran, canola, light olive oil) or melted butter

1 teaspoon vanilla essence

2 cups (330 g/11½ oz) gluten-free plain (all-purpose) flour (see page 15 for recipe)

3 teaspoons gluten-free baking powder

1 teaspoon bicarbonate of soda (baking soda), sifted

½ teaspoon salt

1½ teaspoons ground cinnamon

½ cup (100 g/3½ oz) brown sugar

⅔ cup (65 g/2¼ oz) pecans, roughly chopped

STORAGE
The loaf will keep in the refrigerator, wrapped well in plastic wrap, for up to 5 days, or in the freezer in an airtight container for up to 1 month.

Preheat the oven to 180°C/350°F (160°C/315°F fan-forced) with the oven rack positioned in the middle of the oven.

Grease a 1 kg (2 lb) loaf tin, and line the base and sides with baking paper.

Mix the chia seeds and boiling water together in a small bowl. Set aside for 2–3 minutes to form a gel.

In another bowl, mash the bananas together with a fork. Add the eggs, oil, vanilla and chia gel and whisk together.

Add the dry ingredients to a large bowl and whisk well to combine.

Using a spatula, tip the wet mix into the dry mix and gently fold it through until just mixed. (The mix should still be lumpy.) Fold in the pecans.

Tip the mix into the prepared tin and smooth it out with the back of a spoon.

Lay the banana slices side by side lengthways, cut-side up, on the surface. Press the banana down slightly so it sits flush with the mix.

Bake for approximately 1 hour and 15 minutes, rotating roughly halfway through for even cooking, until a skewer inserted into the centre of the loaf comes out clean or the top springs back when you press down gently on it with two fingers.

Transfer the loaf to a wire rack and leave it to cool slightly for 15–20 minutes before turning out. Slice and serve warm (taking care when cutting as the loaf will still be fragile) or leave to cool completely before serving.

TIPS
- The riper the banana, the sweeter and moister your loaf will be. Using a very ripe banana for the garnish will help it to caramelise while baking.
- While the pecans add a delicious crunch and gentle flavour that complements the banana bread well, they can be replaced with walnuts if you prefer.
- For a decadent banana loaf, break a 200 g (7 oz) bar of dark chocolate into small pieces and fold them into the mix just before tipping it into the tin.

Banana, Blueberry and Coconut Loaf

MAKES 1 LOAF

If you're new to the joys of a freshly baked loaf, this is a good place to start. It's naturally sweet thanks to the overripe bananas and the berries, with a little nuttiness care of the coconut.

3 tablespoons chia seeds

¾ cup (185 ml/6 fl oz) boiling water

5 large overripe bananas (about 475 g/1 lb 1 oz peeled bananas)

3 large eggs, at room temperature

¾ cup (185 ml/6 fl oz) light oil (e.g. sunflower, rice bran, canola, light olive oil) or melted butter

1 teaspoon vanilla essence

2 cups (330 g/11½ oz) gluten-free plain (all-purpose) flour (see page 15 for recipe)

3 teaspoons gluten-free baking powder

1 teaspoon bicarbonate of soda (baking soda), sifted

½ teaspoon salt

1½ teaspoons ground cinnamon

⅔ cup (125 g/4½ oz) brown sugar

½ cup (30 g/1 oz) coconut flakes, plus extra to decorate

1 cup (155 g/5½ oz) fresh or frozen blueberries, plus extra to decorate

Preheat the oven to 180°C/350°F (160°C/315°F fan-forced) with the oven rack positioned in the middle of the oven.

Grease a 1 kg (2 lb) loaf tin and line the base and sides with baking paper.

Mix the chia seeds and boiling water together in a small bowl. Set aside for 2–3 minutes to form a gel.

In another bowl, mash the bananas together with a fork. Add the eggs, oil, vanilla and chia gel and whisk together.

Add the dry ingredients to a large bowl and whisk well to combine.

Using a spatula, tip the wet mix into the dry mix and gently fold it through until just mixed. (The mix should still be lumpy.) Fold in the coconut flakes and blueberries.

Tip the mix into the prepared tin and smooth it out with the back of a spoon. Top with a few extra blueberries and coconut flakes.

Bake for approximately 1 hour and 15 minutes, rotating roughly halfway through for even cooking, until a skewer inserted into the centre of the loaf comes out clean or the top springs back when you press down gently on it with two fingers.

Transfer the loaf to a wire rack and leave it to cool slightly for 15–20 minutes before turning out. Slice and serve warm (taking care when cutting as the loaf will still be fragile) or leave to cool completely before serving.

TIPS

- If using frozen overripe bananas, be sure to defrost them completely before using. Otherwise, your mix will be too cold and the batter won't mix as well, resulting in a dense banana bread.
- Shredded coconut can be substituted for coconut flakes here.

STORAGE

The loaf will keep in the refrigerator, wrapped well in plastic wrap, for up to 5 days.

Banana and Pecan Loaf (page 84),
Banana, Blueberry and Coconut Loaf (page 85)

Lime, Coconut and Yoghurt Loaf with Lime Drizzle

MAKES 1 LOAF

This dairy-free loaf tastes – and looks – as good as it sounds. Perfect for summer when citrus and coconut come into their own.

1½ cups (250 g/9 oz) gluten-free self-raising flour (see page 15 for recipe)

1 teaspoon bicarbonate of soda (baking soda)

1 teaspoon xanthan gum

½ teaspoon salt

½ cup (45 g/1½ oz) desiccated coconut

4 large eggs, at room temperature

1½ cups (330 g/11½ oz) caster (superfine) sugar

135 ml (4½ fl oz) sunflower oil (e.g. sunflower, rice bran, canola, light olive oil)

finely grated zest and juice of 3 limes, plus long strands of zest to decorate

2 teaspoons vanilla extract

2 cups (520 g/1 lb 2 oz) coconut yoghurt

¼ cup (15 g/½ oz) toasted coconut flakes (optional), to decorate

LIME DRIZZLE

2 cups (250 g/9 oz) gluten-free icing (confectioners') sugar, sifted

zest and juice of 2 limes

STORAGE

This loaf doesn't freeze well, but will stay fresh in an airtight container for 3 days or wrapped in plastic wrap in the refrigerator for up to 5 days (allow to return to room temperature before serving).

Preheat the oven to 160°C/315°F (140°C/275°F fan-forced) with the oven rack positioned in the middle of the oven.

Grease a 1 kg (2 lb) loaf tin and line the base and sides with baking paper.

Sift the flour, bicarbonate of soda, xanthan gum and salt into a bowl. Add the desiccated coconut, whisk to combine, and set aside.

Add the eggs and sugar to the bowl of a stand mixer with the whisk attachment and cream together until light and fluffy. (Alternatively, mix the ingredients together in a mixing bowl with a hand mixer.)

Slowly add the oil, lime zest, lime juice and vanilla, and keep mixing until all incorporated, then add the coconut yoghurt and mix to combine. Using the paddle attachment, slowly add the sifted dry ingredients to the bowl in two batches until everything is just mixed together and the flour is completely incorporated.

Pour the mix into the prepared tin, transfer to the oven and bake for approximately 1 hour, rotating roughly halfway through for even cooking, until a skewer inserted into the centre of the loaf comes out clean or the top springs back when you press down gently on it with two fingers.

While the loaf is cooking, make the lime drizzle by mixing the icing sugar, lime zest and lime juice together in a bowl until smooth.

Transfer the loaf to a wire rack and leave to cool slightly for 15–20 minutes before turning out and leaving to cool completely. Once cool, pour the glaze over so it drizzles down the sides, then top with the toasted coconut flakes, if using, and a little extra lime zest. Leave for 10 minutes for the drizzle to set before slicing.

TIPS
- Be sure to use a light-tasting oil, as anything strong will influence the overall flavour.
- For a thicker/thinner drizzle, just add a little more icing sugar or lime juice as preferred.

Zucchini and Walnut Loaf

MAKES 1 LOAF

This recipe requires a bit of a leap of faith – zucchini in a sweet loaf? Well, yes, but the zucchini isn't so much there for taste as it is to provide moisture. The flavour comes from the walnuts and spices. Trust me, it's yum!

1 tablespoon chia seeds

¼ cup (60 ml/2 fl oz) boiling water

4 large eggs, at room temperature

¾ cup (185 ml/6 fl oz) light oil (e.g. sunflower, rice bran, canola, light olive oil) or melted butter

1 teaspoon vanilla essence

2 cups (330 g/11½ oz) gluten-free plain flour (see page 15 for recipe)

2 teaspoons gluten-free baking powder

½ teaspoon bicarbonate of soda (baking soda), sifted

½ teaspoon salt

1½ teaspoons ground cinnamon

1 teaspoon ground nutmeg

¾ cup (150 g/5½ oz) brown sugar

2½ cups (340 g/12 oz) grated zucchini (courgette)

⅔ cup (85 g/3 oz) walnuts, roughly chopped, plus extra to decorate

Preheat the oven to 180°C/350°F (160°C/315°F fan-forced) with the oven rack positioned in the middle of the oven.

Grease a 1 kg (2 lb) loaf tin and line the base and sides with baking paper.

Mix the chia seeds and boiling water together in a small bowl. Set aside for 2–3 minutes to form a gel.

Add the eggs, oil and vanilla to the bowl and whisk together well to break up the chia gel. Set aside.

Add the dry ingredients to a large bowl and whisk well to combine.

Using a spatula, tip the wet mix into the dry mix and gently fold together until just mixed. (The mix should still be lumpy.) Fold in the zucchini and chopped walnuts.

Tip the mix into the prepared tin and smooth it out with the back of a spoon. Top with a few extra chopped walnuts.

Bake for approximately 1 hour and 15 minutes, rotating roughly halfway through for even cooking, until a skewer inserted into the centre of the loaf comes out clean or the top springs back when you press it gently with two fingers.

Transfer the loaf to a wire rack and leave it to cool slightly for 15–20 minutes before turning out. Slice and serve warm with butter (taking care when cutting as the loaf will still be fragile) or leave to cool completely before serving.

TIPS

- The grated zucchini can be replaced with grated carrot, apple or pear, if you prefer, while the walnuts can be replaced with pecans or hazelnuts.
- This loaf is excellent with a lemon or orange drizzle. To make one, simply follow the recipe for lime drizzle on page 88 and replace the lime with a lemon or orange. It also works very well with the addition of ⅔ cup chopped dried fruits (such as dates, prunes, currants, sultanas, raisins or figs).

STORAGE

Refrigerate for up to 5 days or slice and freeze in an airtight container for up to 1 month.

CAKES

When you need to celebrate in style, these cakes won't disappoint. Impressive yet deceptively simple (honestly, anyone can make these), the following recipes are a great thing to have up your sleeve for just such moments.

92–113

Dark Chocolate and Espresso Cake with Mascarpone Cream

SERVES 10–12

In a word, decadent. Chocolate and coffee are one of life's most delicious pairings, combined with the rich creaminess of mascarpone. Perfect for a special occasion.

1¼ cups (125 g/4½ oz) almond meal

⅔ cup (80 g/2¾ oz) coconut flour, sifted

¼ cup (20 g/¾ oz) freshly ground espresso-style coffee, plus extra for decoration

1 teaspoon ground cinnamon

1 teaspoon gluten-free baking powder

⅓ cup (40 g/1½ oz) cocoa powder, sifted

100 g/3½ oz dark chocolate, broken into small chunks, plus extra chocolate for decoration

⅔ cup (170 ml/5½ fl oz) light oil (e.g. sunflower, rice bran, canola, light olive oil) or melted butter

6 large eggs, at room temperature

1¼ cups (220 g/7¾ oz) raw or white caster sugar

2 teaspoons vanilla extract

MASCARPONE CREAM

1 cup (240 g/8½ oz) mascarpone cheese

1 cup (250 ml/9 fl oz) thick (double) cream

¼ cup (30 g/1 oz) gluten-free icing (confectioners') sugar, sifted

Preheat the oven to 160°C/315°F (140°C/275°F fan-forced) with the oven rack positioned in the middle of the oven.

Grease a 24 cm (9½ in) round cake tin and line the base and sides with baking paper.

Whisk the almond meal, coconut flour, coffee, cinnamon, baking powder and cocoa together in a large bowl. Set aside.

Gently warm the chocolate together with the oil in a heavy-based saucepan over low heat until melted but not hot. Set aside.

Add the eggs and sugar to the bowl of a stand mixer with the whisk attachment and cream together until light and fluffy. (Alternatively, mix the ingredients together in a mixing bowl with a hand mixer.) Add the vanilla and melted chocolate mix and lightly whisk to combine.

Using the paddle attachment, slowly add the sifted dry ingredients to the bowl in two batches until everything is just mixed together and the flour is completely incorporated.

Tip the mix into the prepared tin, transfer to the oven and bake for approximately 40 minutes, rotating halfway through cooking, until it's just cooked and barely firm to the touch in the centre (the cake will become firmer as it cools).

Transfer the cake to a wire rack and leave it to cool in the tin for 15 minutes before turning out and leaving to cool completely.

To make the mascarpone cream, gently whisk the mascarpone, cream and icing sugar together in a small bowl until thick and creamy.

Once the cake is cool, slather the mascarpone cream over the top with a spatula. Using a vegetable peeler, create shavings of dark chocolate, and scatter them generously over the cake. Sprinkle over a little ground coffee to finish.

TIP
- As this is quite a rich cake, I recommend to serve it in small slices. The mascarpone cream helps to cut through that richness, so don't be tempted to use whipped cream in its place.

STORAGE

This cake will stay fresh in an airtight container in the fridge for up to 5 days or in the freezer for up to 1 month. When the cake is cold or frozen, it's easier to slice (it will only take around 15 minutes to defrost).

Lemon and Coconut Cake with Lemon Glaze

SERVES 8

Grain- and dairy-free, light, soft and moist – this is one of the most popular lemon cakes we have ever made in the bakery.

⅔ cup (80 g/2¾ oz) coconut flour

1 cup (100 g/3½ oz) almond meal

1 teaspoon baking powder

1 teaspoon ground cinnamon

6 eggs, at room temperature

1⅓ cups (295 g/10½ oz) caster (superfine) sugar

1⅓ cups (330 ml/11¼ fl oz) sunflower oil

1 teaspoon vanilla paste

zest and juice of 2 lemons, plus juice of 1 extra lemon for brushing

toasted coconut flakes, to decorate

LEMON GLAZE

2 cups (250 g/9 oz) gluten-free icing (confectioners') sugar, sifted

¼ cup (60 ml/2 fl oz) lemon juice

Finely grated zest of 1 lemon, plus extra strands of zest to decorate

STORAGE

This cake will stay fresh in an airtight container in the fridge for up to 5 days. It also freezes beautifully – simply wrap the (un-iced) cake in plastic wrap and freeze for up to 1 month, then remove from the freezer when ready to eat and glaze and slice your cake while still frozen for perfect slices (allow 20 minutes to defrost after cutting before serving).

Preheat the oven to 170°C/325°F (150°C/300°F fan-forced) with the oven rack positioned in the middle of the oven.

Grease a 20 cm (8 in) round spring-form cake tin and line the base and sides with baking paper.

Sift the coconut flour, almond meal, baking powder and cinnamon into a bowl and whisk together thoroughly.

Using a stand mixer with the whisk attachment, or in a large bowl with a hand mixer, whisk the eggs and sugar together on high speed until pale and fluffy. Slowly add the oil and vanilla and continue to whisk for 30 seconds more.

Using the paddle attachment on low speed, add the sifted dry ingredients and fold in until everything is mixed together thoroughly, then add the zest and juice of 2 lemons and mix well.

Pour the batter into the prepared tin and smooth the top with the back of a spoon.

Bake for 1 hour 15 minutes, rotating roughly halfway through for even cooking, until the cake is dark golden, a skewer inserted into the centre of the loaf comes out clean, or the cake springs back when you press down gently on the top with two fingers.

Remove the cake from the oven and brush the top with lemon juice. Leave to cool completely in the tin before releasing the spring, removing the sides and peeling away any baking paper as necessary. Remove the cake tin base by sliding the cake onto a serving plate.

Make the lemon glaze by mixing the icing sugar, lemon juice and lemon zest together in a bowl until smooth.

Pour the icing over the top of the cake then use a flat-bladed spatula to quickly smooth the glaze out so it gently tips over the sides to create a drip effect. Decorate with toasted coconut flakes and a little lemon zest. If you want the icing to set (which makes it easier to slice), place the cake in the fridge for 10 minutes before slicing.

TIPS
- If the cake is looking a little dark on top towards the end of the cooking time, don't worry. That's how it should look. It won't be burnt.
- Be sure to sift the dry ingredients – the coconut flour in particular needs it, as it has a tendency to be lumpy and tricky to break down during the mixing process.

Carrot and Orange Cake with Cream Cheese Icing

SERVES 8

Carrot cake is always a crowd-pleaser, especially when it's topped with a luscious cream cheese icing. The buttermilk makes it lovely and light, the walnuts give it texture and the orange provides a little zesty zing.

1 tablespoon chia seeds

¼ cup (60 ml/2 fl oz) boiling water

2 cups (330 g/11½ oz) gluten-free plain (all-purpose) flour (see page 15 for recipe)

½ teaspoon xanthan gum

2 teaspoons gluten-free baking powder

1 teaspoon bicarbonate of soda (baking soda)

½ teaspoon salt

1 teaspoon ground cinnamon

½ teaspoon ground nutmeg

½ teaspoon ground ginger

¼ teaspoon ground cardamom

3 eggs, at room temperature

1 cup (185 g/6½ oz) raw or white caster sugar

½ cup (100 g/3½ oz) brown sugar

⅓ cup (80 ml/2½ fl oz) light oil (e.g. sunflower, rice bran, canola, light olive oil)

1 teaspoon vanilla extract

finely grated zest and juice of 1 orange

½ cup (125 ml/4 fl oz) buttermilk (or non-dairy milk mixed with 2 tablespoons lemon juice)

2 cups (310 g/11 oz) grated carrot

⅔ cup (80 g/2¾ oz) walnuts, chopped plus extra to decorate

Preheat the oven to 170°C/325°F (150°C/300°F fan-forced) with the oven rack positioned in the middle of the oven.

Grease and line two 20 cm (8 in) round cake tins with low sides, and line the base and sides with baking paper.

Mix the chia seeds and boiling water together in a small bowl. Set aside for 2–3 minutes to form a gel.

Sift the flour, xanthan gum, baking powder, bicarbonate of soda, salt and spices together into a large bowl and whisk to combine. Set aside.

Transfer the chia gel to the bowl of a stand mixer fitted with the paddle attachment. Add the eggs, sugars, oil, vanilla, orange zest and orange juice and mix together on low speed. (Alternatively, mix the ingredients together in a mixing bowl with a hand mixer.) Turn off the mixer, add half the flour mix together with half the buttermilk and gently fold in with a spatula. Repeat with the remaining flour mix and buttermilk, being careful not to overmix.

Fold in the carrots and walnuts, then tip the cake mix into the prepared tins and smooth it out with the back of a spoon.

Bake for 40–45 minutes, rotating the tins halfway through for even cooking, until a skewer inserted into the centre of the loaf comes out clean or the top springs back when you press down gently on it with two fingers.

Transfer the cakes to a wire rack and leave them to cool in the tins for 15 minutes before turning out and leaving to cool completely.

continued next page >

CREAM CHEESE ICING

230 g (8 oz) butter, cut into small cubes and softened

230 g (8 oz) cream cheese

2½ cups (310 g/11 oz) gluten-free icing (confectioners') sugar, sifted plus extra if needed

finely grated zest and juice of 1 orange

long strips of zest from 1 orange and 1 lemon, to decorate

STORAGE

Once iced, the carrot cake will keep for 3–4 days in the refrigerator in a suitable airtight container (bring to room temperature to serve). This cake doesn't freeze well.

While the cakes are cooling, make the cream cheese icing. Add the butter, cream cheese, icing sugar and finely grated orange zest and juice to the bowl of a stand mixer fitted with a whisk attachment and cream together on medium–high speed. Taste and add more icing sugar if needed.

Place one cake layer on a serving plate, right side up. Using a spatula, turn out half the icing onto the cake with a spatula and gently spread it out to the edge. Place the second cake on top, right side up, making sure the sides are aligned. Then, using your spatula, turn out the rest of the icing and gently spread it over the top. Scatter the long strips of orange and lemon zest over and top with a few extra chopped walnuts.

TIP
- The xanthan gum helps create the perfect crumb, while the chia gel and buttermilk deliver the lightness that is particularly important for this type of cake (and for gluten-free baking in general). If you can't find buttermilk, substitute milk and lemon juice but be aware that the result won't quite be the same.

Hummingbird Cake with Lemon Cream Icing and Pecans

SERVES 8

Essentially, a hummingbird cake is a banana cake with pineapple and nuts. This cake reminds me of a childhood friend whose mother would bake it (the non-gluten-free version) in summer when mangoes were in season. She'd slather the cake with generous amounts of cream cheese icing then top it with fresh mango. As delicious as that was, this is my version with zesty lemon to replace the mango.

1 tablespoon chia seeds

¼ cup (60 ml/2 fl oz) boiling water

5 large overripe bananas (about 475 g/1 lb 1 oz)

3 large eggs, at room temperature

½ cup (125 ml/4 fl oz) light oil (e.g. sunflower, rice bran, canola, light olive oil) or melted butter

1 teaspoon vanilla extract

2 cups (330 g/11½ oz) gluten-free plain (all-purpose) flour (see page 15 for recipe)

3 teaspoons gluten-free baking powder

1 teaspoon bicarbonate of soda (baking soda), sifted

½ teaspoon salt

1½ teaspoons ground cinnamon

⅓ cup (75 g/2¾ oz) caster sugar

⅓ cup (75 g/2¾ oz) raw sugar

1 cup (260 g/9¼ oz) tinned pineapple pieces

1 cup (190 g/6¾ oz) fresh diced pineapple (optional), to decorate

⅔ cup (65 g/2¼ oz) pecans, roughly chopped, plus extra to decorate

Preheat the oven to 170°C/325°F (150°C/300°F fan-forced) with the oven rack positioned in the middle of the oven.

Grease two 20 cm (8 in) round cake tins with low sides, and line the base and sides with baking paper.

Mix the chia seeds and boiling water together in a small bowl. Set aside for 2–3 minutes to form a gel.

In another bowl, mash the bananas with a fork. Add the eggs, oil, vanilla and chia gel and whisk together.

Add the dry ingredients to a large bowl and whisk well to combine.

Using a spatula, tip the wet mix into the dry mix and gently fold it through until just mixed. (The mix should still be lumpy.) Fold in the pineapple pieces and chopped pecans.

Divide the mix between the prepared tins and smooth it out with the back of a spoon.

Bake for approximately 40-45 minutes, rotating halfway through for even cooking, until a skewer inserted into the centre of the loaf comes out clean or the top springs back when you press it gently with two fingers.

Transfer the cakes to a wire rack and leave them to cool in the tins for 15 minutes before turning out and leaving to cool completely.

LEMON CREAM ICING

230 g (8 oz) butter, cut into small cubes and softened

230 g (8 oz) cream cheese, chopped

2½ cups (310 g/11 oz) gluten-free icing (confectioners') sugar, sifted, plus extra as needed

finely grated zest and juice of 2 lemons

long strips of zest from 2 lemons, to decorate

While the cakes are cooling, make the lemon cream icing. Add the butter, cream cheese and icing sugar to the bowl of a stand mixer fitted with the whisk attachment and cream together on medium–high speed. (Alternatively, mix the ingredients together in a mixing bowl with a hand mixer.) Add the lemon zest and juice, taste and add more icing sugar if needed.

Place one cake layer on a serving plate, right side up. Using a spatula, turn out half the icing onto the cake and gently spread it to the edge. Place your top layer of cake on top, right side up, making sure the sides are aligned. Then, using your spatula, turn out the rest of the icing and gently spread it over the top. Scatter the long strips of lemon zest and fresh pineapple pieces over, and top with a few extra chopped pecans.

STORAGE

Once iced, the hummingbird cake will keep for 3–4 days in the refrigerator in a suitable airtight container (bring to room temperature to serve). This cake doesn't freeze well.

TIPS

- Be sure to use a light-tasting oil, as anything strong will influence the overall taste.
- A lemon drizzle makes a great dairy-free icing alternative for this cake. If you decide to go down this route, there's no need to bake the cake in two tins – instead, bake the mixture in a single high-sided 20 cm (8 in) round tin for approximately 1 hour 15 minutes, then add the drizzle as per the recipe on page 88 – replacing the lime with a lemon – and decorate as above.

Hummingbird Cake with Lemon Cream Icing and Pecans (page 102)

Sponge with Strawberries and Cream

SERVES 8–10

Welcome to my three-ingredient light and fluffy sponge cake. It's easy, but you need to be extra attentive at certain key stages – follow the recipe so you don't miss a trick. You can use this sponge to make so many things, including lamingtons and fruit trifle.

2 punnets (500 g/1 lb 2 oz) ripe strawberries

2 tablespoons caster (superfine) sugar

600 ml (21 fl oz) single (pure) cream or thick (double) cream

gluten-free icing (confectioners') sugar, to dust (optional)

SPONGE

7 large eggs

¾ cup (165 g/5¾ oz) caster (superfine) sugar

⅔ cup (110 g/3¾ oz) gluten-free self-raising flour (see page 15 for recipe)

STORAGE

The creamed sponge will keep for up to 2 days in the fridge. Or the sponge itself, wrapped well, can be frozen for up to 1 month. Serve at room temperature.

Preheat the oven to 180°C/350°F (160°C/315°F fan-forced) with the oven rack positioned in the middle of the oven.

Grease two 20 cm (8 in) shallow round cake tins and line the bases with baking paper.

For the sponge, whisk together the eggs and sugar in a saucepan set over medium heat. Once the mix is hot to the touch (around 65°C/150°F), transfer it to the bowl of a stand mixer with the whisk attachment and whisk for 7–8 minutes, or beat on high speed with a hand mixer until light, creamy and doubled in volume.

Remove the bowl from the mixer and gradually sift in the flour, folding it through gently with a spatula as you go. Continue until all the flour has been added and everything is completely combined, then spoon the batter evenly into the prepared tins and bake for 25–30 minutes, until golden and lightly firm to the touch.

Remove from the oven and leave to cool for 10 minutes in the tins before turning out onto a wire rack and leaving to cool completely. (Expect your sponges to retract from the sides of the cake tin while cooling and shrivel slightly).

While the sponges are cooling, prepare the strawberries and cream. Remove the green stems from the strawberries and slice them thinly lengthways. Place the sliced strawberries in a bowl and scatter the sugar over the top. Shake the bowl to toss the strawberries around and leave to sit for at least 30 minutes. Using a stand mixer with the whisk attachment (or a hand mixer), whip the cream until soft peaks form.

When completely cool, place one sponge on a serving plate. Spread over half the lightly whipped cream and arrange half the strawberry slices on top in an even layer. Top with the second sponge and repeat the process, scattering the strawberries messily over the top and trying to not to press down on the cream on the top layer to keep it soft and peaky. Sift over a little icing sugar to finish.

TIP

- The cream needs to be lightly whipped and soft, but not runny or overwhipped, discoloured or curdled. Single (or pure) cream is quite runny and will need whipping a little longer.

Pear and Polenta Cake with Lemon and Rosemary Syrup

SERVES 8–10

Polenta is a secret weapon in the battle to make fabulous gluten-free cakes, helping to make this citrusy beauty moist and soft.

3 large eggs, at room temperature

½ cup (110 g/3¾ oz) raw sugar, plus 1 tablespoon for sprinkling

230 ml (7¾ fl oz) light oil (e.g. sunflower, rice bran, canola, light olive oil) or melted butter

1 vanilla pod, seeds extracted, or 1 teaspoon vanilla bean extract

zest and juice of 1 lemon

2 cups (200 g/7 oz) almond meal

⅔ cup (125 g/4½ oz) fine polenta

½ cup (85 g/3 oz) gluten-free self-raising flour (see page 15 for recipe)

½ teaspoon salt

2 large ripe pears, 1 peeled and grated, 1 peeled, cored and sliced lengthways into eighths

LEMON AND ROSEMARY SYRUP

zest and juice of 3 lemons

1 teaspoon finely chopped fresh rosemary leaves

½ cup (90 g/3¼ oz) raw or white caster sugar

STORAGE

This cake stays fresh in an airtight container in the fridge for 2–3 days. It does not freeze well.

Preheat the oven to 190°C/375°F (170°C/325°F fan-forced) with the oven rack positioned in the middle of the oven.

Grease a 22 cm (8¾ in) round spring-form cake tin and line the base and sides with baking paper.

Whisk together the eggs, sugar, oil, vanilla and lemon zest and juice in a large bowl.

Add the dry ingredients to a separate large bowl and whisk well to combine.

Using a spatula, tip the wet mix into the dry mix and gently fold it through until just mixed. Fold in the grated pear.

Pour the batter into the prepared tin and smooth it out with the back of a spoon. Fan the pear slices out on top and sprinkle a little raw sugar over.

Bake for approximately 1 hour, rotating roughly halfway through for even cooking, until the cake is golden, a skewer inserted into the centre comes out clean, or the top springs back when you press it gently with two fingers.

While the cake is in the final stages of cooking, make the lemon and rosemary syrup. Place the lemon zest, juice, rosemary and sugar in a saucepan and slowly bring to the boil. Reduce the heat to a simmer and cook for 5–7 minutes, until thickened slightly. Remove from the heat.

When the cake is cooked, remove it from the oven and pour the hot syrup over to cover completely. Leave to sit in the tin for 20 minutes before releasing the spring, removing the sides and peeling away any baking paper as necessary. Gently transfer the cake to a serving plate. Delicious served warm with double cream.

TIPS
- Ripe pears have a higher sugar content and are juicier, caramelising at the base and adding additional moisture to the cake.
- Be sure to use fine polenta, as regular polenta can make the cake a bit gritty.

Baked Cheesecake with Honey Syrup and Gingerbread Crust

SERVES 8–10

New York meets Italy in this delicious baked cheesecake recipe. It has a wonderfully silky, melt-in-your-mouth texture, and a slight tang thanks to the honey syrup with lemon.

250 g (9 oz) Gingerbread Biscuits (see page 62 for recipe)

125 g (4½ oz) butter, melted

500 g (1 lb 2 oz) cream cheese

500 g (1 lb 2 oz) ricotta

¾ cup (165 g/5¾ oz) caster (superfine) sugar

2 teaspoons vanilla extract

4 eggs, at room temperature

HONEY SYRUP

⅔ cup (235 g/8½ oz) honey

1 tablespoon water

juice of ½ lemon

STORAGE

This cheesecake stays fresh in an airtight container in the fridge for up to 3 days. It does not freeze well.

Preheat the oven to 180°C/350°F (160°C/315°F fan-forced) with the oven rack positioned in the middle of the oven.

Grease a 22 cm (8½ in) round spring-form cake tin and line the base and sides with baking paper.

In a food processor, whiz together the gingerbread biscuits for 10–15 seconds to a breadcrumb-like consistency. Add the melted butter and whiz for another 5 seconds, then turn the biscuit base out into the prepared tin and press down on it firmly to make an even layer of crust on the base and up the sides.

Wipe out the food processor, then add the cream cheese, ricotta, sugar, vanilla and eggs and whiz together until smooth. Pour this mix over the top of the gingerbread crust and level it out with a spoon.

Bake the cheesecake for approximately 50 minutes, until the top of the cake is just set and lightly golden. Remove from the oven and leave to cool completely, then transfer to the fridge and leave for 1 hour to chill and set.

For the honey syrup, add all the ingredients to a small saucepan and bring to the boil over medium heat, then reduce the heat to low and simmer gently for 2–3 minutes, until thickened and slightly reduced. Remove from the heat and leave to cool.

When the cheesecake is ready, remove it from the tin and serve with the honey syrup poured over the top.

TIPS

- Although the gingerbread does work deliciously in this recipe, you can replace it with any gluten-free plain biscuit, if you prefer.
- For a richer cheesecake, replace the ricotta with sour cream.

Vanilla, Boysenberry and Lemon Cake with Lemon Syrup

SERVES 8

This is one of my family's all-time favourite cakes, as it showcases some true superstar ingredients – berries, lemon and vanilla. It's light, moist and thoroughly satisfying!

1¾ cups (290 g/10¼ oz) gluten-free plain (all-purpose) flour (see page 15 for recipe)

1½ teaspoons gluten-free baking powder

145 g (5 oz) unsalted butter (or non-dairy alternative), chopped small and at room temperature

¾ cup (165 g/5¾ oz) caster (superfine) sugar

3 eggs, at room temperature

¼ cup (60 ml/2 fl oz) sunflower oil (or other light oil)

1 vanilla pod, seeds extracted (or 1 teaspoon vanilla bean paste)

½ cup (125 ml/4 fl oz) buttermilk (or 100 ml/3½ fl oz) non-dairy milk mixed with 1 tablespoon lemon juice)

250 g (9 oz) boysenberries, halved if large

finely grated zest of 1 lemon

LEMON SYRUP

finely grated zest and juice of 3 lemons

½ cup (110 g/3¾ oz) caster (superfine) sugar

STORAGE

This cake stays fresh in an airtight container in the fridge for up to 2 days. It does not freeze well.

Preheat the oven to 160°C/315°F (140°C/275°F fan-forced) with the oven rack positioned in the middle of the oven.

Grease a 22.5 cm (9 in) round spring-form cake tin or bundt tin. If using a spring-form tin, line the base and sides with baking paper. If using a bundt tin, be generous with the greasing.

Sift the flour and baking powder into a large bowl and whisk to combine. Set aside.

Add the butter and sugar to the bowl of a stand mixer with the paddle attachment fitted and cream together, starting at a low speed and gradually increasing, until pale and creamy. (Alternatively, mix the ingredients in a mixing bowl with a hand mixer.)

Reduce the mixing speed to low–medium and add the eggs one at a time, mixing well after each addition, then add the oil and vanilla and mix until well combined. Turn off the mixer, add half the flour mix together with half the buttermilk and gently fold in. Repeat with the remaining flour mix and buttermilk, being careful not to overmix.

Gently fold in the boysenberries and lemon zest, then tip the cake mix into the prepared tin and smooth it out with the back of a spoon.

Bake for 1 hour, rotating roughly halfway through for even cooking, or until the cake is golden and a skewer inserted into the centre comes out clean, or the top springs back when you press gently on it with two fingers.

While the cake is in the final stages of cooking, make the lemon syrup. Place the lemon zest, juice and sugar into a saucepan and bring to the boil over medium heat. Reduce the heat to a simmer and cook for 5–7 minutes, until thickened slightly. Remove from the heat.

Let the cake sit for 5 minutes to cool. Place a serving plate over the top and flip the tin and plate over to turn the cake out. Pour the hot syrup over to cover completely. Serve warm.

TIPS

- The softer the butter, the quicker the butter and sugar will become pale and creamy, so be careful not to over-cream the mix! This is especially the case when using non-dairy butter.
- Using fresh vanilla or vanilla paste will not only enhance the flavour but also give you lovely flecks of vanilla seeds through the cake batter.

PASTRY, TARTS
and PIES

These are the recipes I turn to when I have a bit of time –
not because they are hard, but because pastry is an involved
process that benefits from thought and attention.
It's always worth it. The rewards are amazing!

114–131

Sweet Decadent Shortcrust Pastry

MAKES 1 KG (2 LB 4 OZ)

It's not easy working without the elasticity that gluten provides, but after much experimentation I've developed a recipe that will give you a beautiful result. You just need to follow the golden rules of any pastry making – so please read my tips, opposite, before you get started.

2⅔ cups (440 g/15½ oz) gluten-free plain (all-purpose) flour (see page 15 for recipe), plus extra for dusting

2½ teaspoons xanthan gum

⅓ cup (75 g/2¾ oz) caster (superfine) sugar

335 g (11¾ oz) cold unsalted butter, cut into small cubes

⅓ cup (85 g/3 oz) sour cream

1 large egg, at room temperature

STORAGE

Uncooked pastry dough can be kept refrigerated for up to 1 week or frozen for up to 1 month. Any excess unused dough should be flattened to no more than 3 cm (1¼ in) thick (it's easier to roll once thawed) and wrapped well in plastic wrap for later use. If frozen, simply defrost in the refrigerator and use while cold.

Add the flour, xanthan gum and sugar to a food processor and whiz together for 10 seconds. Add the butter and mix for 30 seconds, until the mixture resembles breadcrumbs, then add the sour cream and egg and mix for 10 seconds, until the dough comes together and forms a ball.

Turn the soft dough out on a sheet of plastic wrap and wrap well, flattening the dough out to a disc 2 cm (¾ in) thick. Rest the dough by chilling in the fridge for at least 1 hour, ideally overnight. (This will make it easier to work with – day-old pastry always works best!)

Once rested, unwrap the dough, transfer it to a floured surface (using gluten-free flour) and leave it for 2–3 minutes to soften. Using a floured rolling pin (using gluten-free flour), work the dough by rolling it out, folding it back on itself and then rolling it out again. Repeat this process a few times, then roll the pastry out to a 2 cm (¾ in) thickness, rewrap and chill until needed.

When you're ready to use your dough, unwrap it and leave it on a lightly floured bench for 2–3 minutes to warm up. Once the pastry has softened slightly, rub a little flour over the surface.

Using a lightly floured rolling pin, roll the pastry out as required, rolling it a few times one way, then flipping it over and re-flouring the bench and rolling pin as necessary. (The trick here is not to over-flour the pastry as this will dry it out – just add as much as you need so the dough is workable and doesn't stick to the bench.)

Using a fork or a pastry docker, lightly stab the pastry to indent it all over. (This process helps prevent the pastry from rising and keeps it flat and even while baking.)

Now the pastry is ready for cutting out and/or lining. When using a cutter, make sure the cutter it is lightly floured, so it doesn't stick to the pastry. When lining, grease the tart or pie tin/dish with butter or a spray oil and always cut your pastry so it's oversized before you line it, then gently let the pastry fall into the tin/dish – this way, you can cut the excess pastry once you've finished and have less shrinkage when baking. Don't stretch the pastry, as it will become too thin and fall apart.

If the pastry is going to be filled then baked, there is no need to parbake it first. If you are planning on finishing it with fresh ingredients, then bake it at 180°C/350°F (160°C/320°F fan-forced) until golden. Leave in the tin to cool completely.

TIPS

- Pastry dough needs to be worked fast, as it's easier to manage when cold. Working the dough and touching it with your warm hands will make it difficult to handle.
- When lining a tart tin, always use one with a removable base. The best way to bake your tart is to line a flat baking tray with baking paper, then place the greased and lined tart ring on top (do not use the removable tart base). That way, it's easier to check if the underside of the pastry is cooked. Simply use a spatula to gently lift the tart slightly to check the pastry. When it's golden, it's cooked.

Sweet Dairy-free Shortcrust Pastry

MAKES 1KG (2 LB 4 OZ)

The golden rule of working fast with pastry is doubly true for dairy-free pastry. Make sure your margarine is cold to start with and re-chill the dough if it gets too soft.

2⅔ cups (440 g/15½ oz) gluten-free plain (all-purpose) flour (see page 15 for recipe)

2½ teaspoons xanthan gum

⅓ cup (75 g/2¾ oz) caster (superfine) sugar

420 g (15 oz) cold hard cooking vegan margarine, cut into small cubes

1 large egg, lightly beaten

STORAGE

Uncooked pastry dough can be refrigerated for up to 1 week or frozen for up to 1 month. Any excess unused dough should be flattened to no more than 3 cm (1¼ in) thick and wrapped well in plastic wrap. If frozen, simply defrost in the refrigerator and use while cold.

Add the flour, xanthan gum and sugar to a food processor and whiz together for 10 seconds. Add the margarine and mix for 15 seconds, until the mixture resembles breadcrumbs, then add the egg and mix for 10 seconds, until soft.

Turn the soft, sticky dough out on a sheet of plastic wrap and wrap well, flattening the dough to a disc 2 cm (¾ in) thick. Rest the dough by chilling in the fridge for at least 1 hour, ideally overnight. (This will make it easier to work with – day-old pastry always works best!)

When you're ready to use your dough, unwrap it and leave it on a lightly floured bench for 2–3 minutes to warm up. Once the pastry has softened slightly, rub a little flour over the surface.

Place the dough on floured baking paper and roll it out using a floured rolling pin, folding it back on itself and then rolling it out again. Repeat this process a few times over, re-flouring the bench and rolling pin as necessary, then roll it out to the required thickness. (The trick here is not to over-flour the pastry as this will dry it out – just add as much as you need so the dough is workable.)

Using a fork or a pastry docker, lightly stab the pastry to indent it all over. (This process helps prevent the pastry from rising and keeps it flat and even while baking.)

Now the pastry is ready for cutting out and/or lining. When using a cutter, make sure it is lightly floured, so it doesn't stick to the pastry. When lining, grease the tart or pie tin/dish with margarine or a spray oil and always cut your pastry so it's oversized before you line it, then gently let the pastry fall into the tin/dish – this way, you can cut the excess pastry once you've finished and have less shrinkage when baking. Don't stretch the pastry, as it will become too thin and fall apart.

If the pastry is going to be filled then baked, there is no need to parbake it first. If you are planning on finishing it with fresh ingredients, then bake it at 180°C/350°F (160°C/320°F fan-forced) until golden. Leave to cool completely before filling or removing from the tart ring.

TIP
- Margarine can be very difficult to work with, as it softens quickly. If the pastry becomes too soft while rolling, simply chill it again until it's cool enough to handle.

Mixed Berry Frangipane Tart

SERVES 6

Frangipane is a wonderful almond pastry filling that's quick and easy to make but incredibly versatile. It's nutty, creamy and sweet, making it the perfect base for berries or other fruits, including figs and nectarines.

250 g (9 oz) Sweet Decadent Shortcrust Pastry (see page 116), pre-worked, chilled and docked

1½ cups (225 g/8 oz) fresh or frozen berries or seasonal fruit of choice

handful of flaked almonds, to decorate (optional)

gluten-free icing (confectioners') sugar, to dust

FRANGIPANE

125 g (4½ oz) unsalted butter, chopped and at room temperature

½ cup (110 g/3¾ oz) caster (superfine) sugar

1¼ cups (125 g/4½ oz) almond meal

½ teaspoon vanilla extract

splash of rum (optional)

3 eggs, at room temperature

To make the frangipane, using a stand mixer with the paddle attachment fitted (or a hand mixer), cream the butter for 2–3 minutes until softened and pale. Mix in the sugar, then the almond meal, vanilla and rum, if using. Add the eggs one at a time, mixing well after each addition. Set aside.

Preheat the oven to 190°C/375°F (170°C/325°F fan-forced) with the oven rack positioned in the middle of the oven.

Line a baking tray with baking paper.

Remove the base of a 20 x 3 cm (8 x 1¼ in) loose-bottomed quiche tin and place the ring on the lined tray. Grease with a spray oil or butter.

Place the chilled and pre-worked pastry on a floured surface. Using a rolling pin, roll the pastry out into a 27 cm (10¾ in) disc approximately 3 mm (⅛ in) thick. Gently place the pastry over the quiche ring and let it fall into the tin, allowing it to drape over the top edge. Lightly press the pastry into the shape of the tin, making sure it's pressed flush with the top of the ring so it looks neat.

Fill the tart shell with the frangipane mix and gently level out with the back of a spoon, then top with the fresh or frozen berries or seasonal fruit. Scatter the flaked almonds over, if using.

Bake for 35–40 minutes or until the filling is golden brown and firm to the touch and the pastry is golden underneath. (To check this, slide a spatula under the pastry and lift it slightly to take a look.)

Once cooked, remove from the oven and leave to cool slightly on the tray, then slide off the ring and transfer the tart to a plate. Dust with icing sugar and serve warm or at room temperature.

STORAGE

Frangipane tart can be stored in the refrigerator for 3–4 days or frozen in an airtight container for up to 1 month. Simply defrost and eat at room temperature or reheat and serve warm.

TIPS

- While making frangipane is a quick process, be sure not to overwork it. It's really easy for the frangipane to split as you go, but having all the cold ingredients at room temperature will help to prevent this. I prefer to make frangipane a day ahead of time, as it works best when it's at least 1 day old.
- I love to use berries here, as they don't need any chopping or pre-cooking. Sweet and ripe stone fruits or fresh figs also work well.

Pear and Hazelnut Chocolate Frangipane Tart

SERVES 6

Pear and chocolate are a marriage made in culinary heaven. Add in the nuttiness of hazelnuts and almonds, and you have a beautiful dessert guaranteed to impress.

250 g (9 oz) Sweet Decadent Shortcrust Pastry (see page 116), pre-worked, chilled and docked

500 g (1 lb 2 oz) tinned or freshly poached pear halves, cut into 1 cm (½ in) thick slices

handful of hazelnuts, chopped, to decorate (optional)

gluten-free icing (confectioners') sugar, to dust

HAZELNUT CHOCOLATE FRANGIPANE

125 g (4½ oz) unsalted butter, cut into small cubes, at room temperature

⅔ cup (150 g/5½ oz) caster (superfine) sugar

1 cup (100 g/3½ oz) hazelnut meal

½ teaspoon vanilla extract

⅓ cup (40 g/1½ oz) cocoa powder, sifted

splash of rum (optional)

3 large eggs, at room temperature

STORAGE

Frangipane tart can be stored in the refrigerator for 3–4 days or frozen in an airtight container for up to 1 month. Simply defrost and eat at room temperature or reheat and serve warm.

To make the frangipane, using a stand mixer with the paddle attachment fitted (or a hand mixer), cream the butter for 2–3 minutes until softened and pale. Mix in the sugar, then the hazelnut meal, vanilla, cocoa and rum, if using. Add the eggs one at a time, mixing well after each addition. Set aside.

Preheat the oven to 190°C/375°F (170°C/325°F fan-forced) with the oven rack positioned in the middle of the oven.

Remove the base of a 20 x 3 cm (8 x 1¼ in) loose-bottomed quiche tin and place the ring on the lined tray. Grease with a spray oil or butter.

Place the chilled and pre-worked pastry on a floured surface. Using a rolling pin, roll the pastry out into a 27 cm (10¾ in) disc approximately 3 mm (⅛ in) thick. Gently place the pastry over the quiche ring and let it fall into the tin, allowing it to drape over the top edge. Lightly press the pastry into the shape of the tin, making sure it's pressed flush with the top of the ring so it looks neat.

Fill the tart shell with the frangipane mix and gently level out with the back of a spoon, then top with the pear slices. (I like to place them with the centres facing down and fanned around the tart so when the frangipane cooks and rises around the pears, it doesn't cover them.) Scatter the chopped hazelnuts over, if using.

Bake for 35–40 minutes or until the filling is golden brown and firm to the touch and the pastry is golden underneath. (To check this, slide a spatula under the pastry and lift it slightly to take a look.)

Once cooked, remove from the oven and leave to cool slightly on the tray, then slide off the ring and transfer the tart to a plate. Serve warm or at room temperature, dusted with a little icing sugar.

TIP
- While tinned pears work excellently in this recipe, you can use freshly poached pears if you prefer. If using fresh pears, make sure they're ripe, soft and sweet – I like to lightly poach mine with lemon peel and cinnamon quills, which give a gentle flavour to the tart.

Lemon Tart

SERVES 8

Or *tarte au citron*, if you want to be fancy. This is a classic, but there's nowhere to hide – the pastry has to be short without being too crumbly and the lemon filling luscious and tangy but not too tart. You will achieve both with this recipe if you follow each step carefully.

500 g (1 lb 2 oz) Sweet Decadent Shortcrust Pastry (see page 116), pre-worked, chilled and docked

LEMON FILLING

4 large eggs, at room temperature

1¼ cups (275 g/9¾ oz) caster (superfine) sugar

200 ml (7 fl oz) lemon juice (from 6–8 lemons)

175 g (6 oz) unsalted butter, cut into small cubes, at room temperature

Lemon zest, for serving

STORAGE

Lemon tart is best stored in an airtight container in the refrigerator for 3–4 days or frozen for up to 2 weeks. Simply defrost and eat at room temperature.

Line a baking tray with baking paper.

Remove the base of a 26 x 3 cm (10¼ x 1¼ in) loose-bottomed quiche tin and place the ring on the lined tray. Grease with a spray oil or butter.

Place the chilled and pre-worked pastry on a floured surface. Using a rolling pin, roll the pastry out into a 36 cm (14 in) disc approximately 3 mm (⅛ in) thick. Gently place the pastry over the quiche ring and let it fall into the tin, allowing it to drape over the top edge. Lightly press the pastry into the shape of the tin, making sure it comes approximately 4 mm (³⁄₁₆ in) above the tart ring edge – this way, you'll have less shrinkage when baking. Don't stretch the pastry too thin or it will fall apart. Chill the pastry for 30 minutes.

Preheat the oven to 180°C/350°F (160°C/315°F fan-forced) with the oven rack positioned in the middle of the oven.

Bake the pastry for 25–30 minutes, until golden. Remove from the oven and leave to cool on the baking tray.

To make the lemon filling, using a stand mixer with the whisk attachment or a hand mixer, mix the eggs and sugar together for 30 seconds. Add the lemon juice and continue to mix for 15 seconds.

Pour the mix into a large saucepan over low heat and slowly bring to the boil, whisking constantly to avoid the mixture sticking and burning on the bottom of the pan. Add the butter and whisk together briefly until smooth, then immediately pour into the cooled tart shell.

Transfer the tart to the refrigerator and leave to chill for 1 hour, or until set. Garnish with lemon zest. The tart is delicious served on its own or with cream.

TIP

- Pastry always works better when it has a chance to chill and rest – where possible, I like to make it a day ahead. Rolling out the pastry to 3 mm (⅛ in) thick will ensure a nice thin, crisp end result rather than a thick pastry that takes over the entire flavour of the tart.

Strawberry Tart

SERVES 8

I've never met anyone who doesn't love a strawberry tart. It's fresh and light but indulgent thanks to the creamy, sweet crème pâtissière.

500 g (1 lb 2 oz) Sweet Decadent Shortcrust Pastry (see page 116), pre-worked, chilled and docked

2–3 punnets (500–750 g/ 1 lb 2 oz–1 lb 10 oz) large strawberries, tops trimmed, halved

EASY CRÈME PÂTISSIÈRE

800 ml (28 fl oz) milk

2 teaspoons vanilla paste

8 egg yolks, at room temperature

⅔ cup (150 g/5½ oz) caster (superfine) sugar

⅔ cup (85 g/3 oz) gluten-free cornflour (cornstarch), sifted

STORAGE

Strawberry tart will keep stored in the refrigerator in an airtight container for 1–2 days.

Line a baking tray with baking paper.

Remove the base of a 26 x 3 cm (10 x 1¼ in) loose-bottomed quiche tin and place the ring on the lined tray. Grease with a spray oil or butter.

Place the chilled and pre-worked pastry on a floured surface. Using a rolling pin, roll the pastry out into a 36 cm (14 in) disc approximately 3 mm (⅛ in) thick. Gently place the pastry over the quiche ring and let it fall into the tin, allowing it to drape over the top edge. Lightly press the pastry into the shape of the tin, making sure it comes approximately 4 mm (³⁄₁₆ in) above the edge – this way, you'll have less shrinkage when baking. Don't stretch the pastry too thin or it will fall apart. Chill the pastry for 30 minutes.

Preheat the oven to 180°C/350°F (160°C/315°F fan-forced) with the oven rack positioned in the middle of the oven.

Place the pastry in the oven and bake for 20–25 minutes, until golden. Remove and leave to cool on the baking tray.

To make the crème pâtissière, heat the milk and vanilla together in a saucepan over medium heat until just simmering.

In a separate saucepan, whisk the egg and sugar together over low heat until thick. Whisk in the milk to combine, then add the cornflour and whisk constantly, being careful not to burn the bottom, until the mixture has thickened to the consistency of thick custard. Remove from the heat.

While still hot, pour the crème pâtissière into a large plastic container lined with plastic wrap and cover with a layer of plastic wrap directly on the surface so a skin doesn't form. Refrigerate to set.

Once set, remove from the refrigerator and tip into the bowl of a stand mixer with the whisk attachment (alternatively, use a large bowl and a hand mixer). Whisk the crème pâtissière for 1 minute, or until it's soft and smooth, then tip it into the cooled pastry shell and level the surface with a large metal spatula.

Starting from the outside and working your way in, top the tart with the strawberry halves. Refrigerate until ready to serve.

TIP
- The strawberries can be replaced with any other fresh berries or seasonal fruit.

Apple and Cinnamon Pie

SERVES 8

A delicious, piping hot home-made apple pie is guaranteed to make people feel nurtured and happy. Use any apples you like and enjoy this with a dollop of ice cream or dairy-free coconut yoghurt.

1 egg, beaten

1 teaspoon water

1 kg (2 lb 4 oz) Sweet Decadent Shortcrust Pastry (see page 116), pre-worked and chilled

1 tablespoon caster (superfine) sugar

FILLING

juice of 1 lemon

1 kg (2 lb 4 oz) apples, peeled, cored and thinly sliced

¾ cup (165 g/5¾ oz) caster (superfine) sugar

1½ teaspoons ground cinnamon

½ teaspoon ground nutmeg

pinch of salt

1 teaspoon vanilla extract

2 tablespoons gluten-free plain (all-purpose) flour (see page 15 for recipe)

STORAGE

This apple pie can be stored in the refrigerator in an airtight container for 3–4 days or frozen for up to 1 month. Simply defrost, reheat and serve warm.

For the filling, add the lemon juice and apple pieces to a large mixing bowl and toss together to coat the apple pieces evenly. In a small mixing bowl, whisk together the sugar, spices, salt, vanilla and flour. Add this mix to the apples and toss to coat.

Preheat the oven to 180°C/350°F (160°C/315°F fan-forced) with the oven rack positioned in the middle of the oven.

Grease a circular 23 x 4.5 cm (9 x 1¾ in) deep pie or cake tin.

Mix the egg and water together with a fork and set aside.

Place the chilled and pre-worked pastry on a floured surface. Using a rolling pin, roll the pastry out into a 36 cm (14 in) disc approximately 4 mm (¼ in) thick.

Prick the pastry with a docker or a fork, then transfer to the pie tin either by rolling the pastry disc onto a rolling pin or simply moving it carefully and quickly with your hands. Place the pastry over the pie tin very gently and let it fall into the dish, bringing it in from the outside edges. Gently press the pastry evenly around the base and sides of the dish. Cut the excess pastry from the outside rim with a small sharp knife and set aside.

Evenly fill the pie shell with the apple mix. Brush the edge of the pastry with the beaten egg mix (this will help glue down the top of the pastry).

Reroll the remaining pastry into a disc big enough to cover the top of the pie and approximately 3mm (⅛ in) thick. Gently place it over the top of the pie, pressing down the edges to seal. Trim away any excess pastry, then glaze the top of the pie with the remaining egg mix using a pastry brush. Sprinkle the caster sugar over the pie and, using your knife, carefully cut a pie hole or some slits into the pastry as vents.

Place the pie in the oven and bake for 45–50 minutes, until golden brown.

Once cooked, remove from the oven and allow to cool slightly. Serve warm or cold with ice cream or cream.

TIP

- You can use pretty much any apples you like. Just be sure to slice them thinly so that they cook through as the pie is baking.

Fruit Mince Pies

MAKES 12

For me, Christmas isn't Christmas without fruit mince pies, but even if you don't celebrate it, you can still enjoy these treats any time. I love filling the house with the divine aroma of spices, fruit and sherry bubbling away. These make great gifts, too, so make a few extra while you're at it.

1 egg, beaten

1 teaspoon water

1 kg (2 lb 4 oz) Sweet Decadent Shortcrust Pastry (see page 116), pre-worked and chilled

2–3 tablespoons caster (superfine) sugar

FRUIT MINCE

3 large apples, grated

½ cup (85 g/3 oz) raisins

1 cup (140 g/5 oz) currants

finely grated zest of 1 orange

½ cup (100 g/3½ oz) brown sugar

½ teaspoon ground cinnamon

½ teaspoon ground nutmeg

¼ teaspoon ground cloves

¼ teaspoon ground allspice

¼ cup (60 ml/2 fl oz) orange juice, plus extra ½ cup for cornflour

⅔ cup (170 ml/5½ fl oz) white wine

⅔ cup (170 ml/5½ fl oz) sherry

¼ cup (30 g/1 oz) gluten-free cornflour (cornstarch)

STORAGE

These pies can be stored at room temperature in an airtight container for 4–5 days or frozen for 1 month. Defrost and serve at room temperature or reheat.

For the fruit mince, place all the ingredients except the cornflour in a saucepan. Bring to the boil over medium heat, then reduce the heat to low and simmer for 20–25 minutes, until the liquid has reduced by about half.

Whisk the cornflour into the orange juice, then pour into the fruit mince mix, and stir so there are no lumps. Remove from the heat and set aside to cool. Once it's cooled, give it a good mix with a large spoon.

Preheat the oven to 190°C/375°F (170°C/325°F fan-forced) with the oven rack positioned in the middle of the oven.

Grease a 12-hole ½-cup muffin tray with butter or lightly spray with oil.

In a small bowl, mix the egg and water together with a fork.

Place the chilled and pre-worked pastry on a floured surface. Using a rolling pin, roll the pastry out into a disk approximately 3 mm (⅛ in) thick.

Prick the pastry with a docker or a fork, then, using a biscuit cutter approximately 10.5 cm (4¼ in) in diameter, cut out 12 pastry bottoms. Reroll the remaining pastry to the same thickness and cut out 12 pastry tops with an 8.5 cm (3¼ in) circular cutter.

Taking one pastry bottom, place it over one of the muffin tin holes and very gently let the pastry fall into it, gently pressing the pastry evenly around the base and sides of hole. Press the top outer edge of the pastry out slightly for the pastry tops to stick to. Repeat with the remaining pastry bottoms.

Evenly fill the pie shells with the cooled fruit mix. Brush the edges of the pastry shells with the beaten egg mix (this will help glue the top of the pastry) then gently cover with the pastry tops and press down on the edges to seal. Glaze the tops of the pies with the remaining egg mix using a pastry brush and sprinkle the sugar over. With a skewer, pierce a hole in the top of each pie to act as a vent.

Bake for 25–30 minutes, or until just starting to brown.

Remove from the oven and allow to cool slightly. Delicious served warm or at room temperature.

PART *TWO*
savoury

MUFFINS
134

SCONES and PANCAKES
148

PASTRY, QUICHES and PIES
160

MUFFINS

Just like their sweet counterparts, savoury muffins are
great grab-and-go bakes and are very popular at the bakery.
Warm straight out of the oven, for breakfast, lunch or
as an afternoon snack – they go across the day in
a way nothing else quite does.

134–147

Spinach, Feta, Cherry Tomato and Dill Muffins

MAKES 6 LARGE MUFFINS

I'm harnessing the power of that age-old combination of cheese and veg in this recipe. Feta has a lovely tanginess that brings out the earthy flavour of spinach.

1 tablespoon chia seeds

¼ cup (60 ml/2 fl oz) boiling water

1½ cups (70 g/2½ oz) baby spinach leaves, chopped

½ cup (125 ml/4 fl oz) light oil (e.g. sunflower, rice bran, canola, light olive oil) or melted butter, plus extra for sautéing

2 eggs

1 cup (250 ml/9 fl oz) full-cream milk (or non-dairy alternative)

1⅔ cups (275 g/9¾ oz) gluten-free self-raising flour (see page 15 for recipe)

¼ teaspoon bicarbonate of soda (baking soda), sifted

1 teaspoon salt

½ teaspoon cracked black pepper

½ teaspoon ground nutmeg

½ cup (70 g/2½ oz) finely chopped feta, plus extra to garnish

½ cup (70 g/2½ oz) cherry tomatoes, quartered, plus extra to garnish

1 tablespoon chopped fresh dill, plus extra to garnish

Preheat the oven to 190°C/375°F (170°C/325°F fan-forced) with the oven rack positioned in the middle of the oven.

Line a large 6-hole muffin tin with high-sided muffin wraps (or grease the tin with a little butter or oil if not using papers).

Mix the chia seeds and boiling water together in a small bowl. Set aside for 2–3 minutes to form a gel.

In a non-stick frying pan, lightly sauté the spinach in a little extra oil until just wilted. Remove from the heat and set aside.

Whisk the eggs, oil and milk together in a separate bowl. Tip in the chia gel and whisk again to break up the gel. Set aside.

Add the dry ingredients to a large bowl and whisk well to combine.

Using a spatula, tip the wet mix into the dry mix and gently fold it through until just combined. (The mix should still be lumpy.) Add the sautéed spinach, feta, tomatoes and dill, and gently fold in until just mixed.

Using a ¼ cup spring-loaded ice-cream scoop, take a flat scoop of mix and empty it into a muffin tin. Repeat the process so you have two scoops per muffin wrap. (The mix should be about two-thirds of the way up each muffin wrap, leaving enough room for the muffins to rise.)

Garnish the top of each muffin with a few pieces of feta, a couple of tomato quarters and a light sprinkling of dill. Transfer to the oven and bake for approximately 20 minutes, then rotate the tray and continue to bake for a further 8–10 minutes, or until the muffins are lightly golden and a skewer inserted into the centre of each comes out clean.

Remove the muffins from the oven and leave to cool in the tin for 10 minutes before turning out onto a wire rack. Serve warm or at room temperature.

STORAGE

These muffins will keep stored in an airtight container in the refrigerator for up to 3 days, or in the freezer for up to 1 month.

TIPS

- Frozen cooked spinach, thawed and thoroughly squeezed to weigh 100 g (3½ oz), can replace the sautéed spinach here if you prefer.
- Be sure to use fresh dill, as its flavour is far milder than that of dried dill, which is too pungent.
- Removing the muffins from the tin to cool completely prevents them from sweating in the tin and going soggy.

Mushroom, Kale, Parmesan, Chilli and Basil Muffins

MAKES 6 LARGE MUFFINS

Yes, there are a few ingredients to get for this recipe, but trust me, it's worth the effort. They absolutely sing together. Serve warm for a delicious breakfast or snack.

1 tablespoon chia seeds

¼ cup (60 ml/2 fl oz) boiling water

1½ cups (135 g/4¾ oz) thinly sliced button or field mushrooms

1 cup (65 g/2¼ oz) finely shredded kale leaves

1 long red chilli, finely sliced

½ cup (125 ml/4 fl oz) oil of choice (e.g. sunflower, rice bran, canola, light olive oil) or melted butter, plus extra for sautéing

2 eggs

1 cup (250 ml/9 fl oz) full-cream milk (or non-dairy alternative)

1⅔ cups (275 g/9¾ oz) gluten-free self-raising flour (see page 15 for recipe)

¼ teaspoon bicarbonate of soda (baking soda), sifted

1 teaspoon salt

½ teaspoon cracked black pepper

½ cup (50 g/1¾ oz) grated parmesan, plus extra to garnish

10 fresh basil leaves, finely shredded, plus extra to garnish

Preheat the oven to 190°C/375°F (170°C/325°F fan-forced) with the oven rack positioned in the middle of the oven.

Line a large 6-hole muffin tin with high-sided muffin wraps (or grease the tin with a little butter or oil if not using papers).

Mix the chia seeds and boiling water together in a small bowl. Set aside for 2–3 minutes to form a gel.

In a non-stick frying pan, lightly sauté the mushrooms in a little extra oil over medium heat for 5 minutes until lightly golden. Add the kale and chilli and continue to sauté for 2–3 minutes more, then remove from the heat and set aside.

Whisk the eggs, oil and milk together in a separate bowl. Tip in the chia gel and whisk again to break up the gel. Set aside.

Add the dry ingredients to a large bowl and whisk well to combine.

Using a spatula, tip the wet mix into the dry mix and gently fold it through until just combined. (The mix should still be lumpy.) Add the mushroom mixture together with the parmesan and shredded basil, and gently fold in until just mixed.

Using a ¼ cup spring-loaded ice-cream scoop, take a flat scoop of mix and empty it into a muffin tin. Repeat the process so you have two scoops per muffin wrap. (The mix should be about two-thirds of the way up each muffin wrap, leaving enough room for the muffins to rise.)

Garnish the top of each muffin with a sprinkle of parmesan and a little shredded basil. Transfer to the oven and bake for approximately 20 minutes. Rotate the tray and continue to bake for a further 10 minutes, or until the muffins are lightly golden and a skewer inserted into the centre of each comes out clean.

Remove the muffins from the oven and leave to cool in the tin for 10 minutes before turning out onto a wire rack. Serve warm or at room temperature.

STORAGE

These muffins will keep stored in an airtight container in the refrigerator for up to 3 days, or in the freezer for up to 1 month.

TIPS

- To shred basil, simply pull the leaves off the stem and pile them on top of one another. Shred the leaves with a sharp knife, making sure not to bruise them, so they stay green, rather than turn black.
- To reduce the spiciness of these muffins, discard the seeds before slicing the chilli.

GLUTEN-FREE BAKING MADE SIMPLE

Zucchini, Caramelised Onion, Parmesan and Thyme Muffins

MAKES 6 LARGE MUFFINS

Whenever I see a recipe with caramelised onion in it, I know it's going to be full of flavour. Parmesan provides sharpness, zucchini delivers moisture, and there's a hint of fresh thyme to balance everything off. This is a great muffin to have with a soup or salad.

2 teaspoons olive oil

2 brown onions, thinly sliced

1 tablespoon chia seeds

¼ cup (60 ml/2 fl oz) boiling water

2 eggs

½ cup (125 ml/4 fl oz) light oil (e.g. sunflower, rice bran, canola, light olive oil) or melted butter

1 cup (250 ml/9 fl oz) full-cream milk (or non-dairy alternative)

1⅔ cups (275 g/9¾ oz) gluten-free self-raising flour (see page 15 for recipe)

¼ teaspoon bicarbonate of soda (baking soda), sifted

1 teaspoon salt

½ teaspoon cracked black pepper

½ teaspoon ground nutmeg

¾ cup (100 g/3½ oz) finely grated zucchini (courgette), plus extra slices to garnish

½ cup (50 g/1¾ oz) grated parmesan, plus extra to garnish

1 tablespoon fresh thyme leaves, plus extra to garnish

Preheat the oven to 190°C/375°F (170°C/325°F fan-forced) with the oven rack positioned in the middle of the oven.

Line a large 6-hole muffin tin with high-sided muffin wraps (or grease the tin with a little butter or oil if not using papers).

Warm a non-stick frying pan over low heat. Add the olive oil and onions and sauté for 25–30 minutes, until caramelised. Set aside to cool completely.

Mix the chia seeds and boiling water together in a small bowl. Set aside for 2–3 minutes to form a gel.

Whisk the eggs, oil and milk together in a separate bowl. Tip in the chia gel and whisk again to break up the gel. Set aside.

Add the dry ingredients to a large bowl and whisk well to combine.

Using a spatula, tip the wet mix into the dry mix and gently fold it through until just combined. (The mix should still be lumpy.) Add the zucchini, caramelised onion, parmesan and thyme leaves, and gently fold in until just mixed.

Using a ¼ cup spring-loaded ice-cream scoop, take a flat scoop of the mix and empty it into a muffin tin. Repeat the process so you have two scoops per muffin wrap. (The mix should be about two-thirds of the way up each muffin wrap, leaving room for the muffins to rise.)

Garnish the top of each muffin with a few zucchini slices, a little grated parmesan and a few thyme leaves. Transfer to the oven and bake for approximately 20 minutes. Rotate the tray and continue to bake for a further 10 minutes, or until the muffins are lightly golden and a skewer inserted into the centre of each comes out clean.

Remove the muffins from the oven and leave to cool in the tin for 10 minutes before turning out onto a wire rack. Serve warm or at room temperature.

STORAGE

These muffins will keep stored in an airtight container in the refrigerator for up to 3 days, or in the freezer for up to 1 month.

TIPS

- It's really important to caramelise the onions rather than just fry them off – you're after the sweetness they develop when cooked slowly, as it's what makes these muffins so delicious.
- A nice, sharp parmesan is essential for offsetting the other flavours. Other sharp cheeses that would work well include pecorino romano, vintage cheddar and manchego.

Roast Sweet Potato, Zucchini, Feta and Rosemary Muffins

MAKES 6 LARGE MUFFINS

I love the combination of ingredients in these savoury muffins – the caramelised sweet potato, sharp salty feta and fragrant, woody rosemary deliver a hit of contrasting flavours with every bite.

1 sweet potato (about 140 g/ 5 oz), cut into 1 cm (½ in) cubes

1 teaspoon olive oil

1 tablespoon chia seeds

¼ cup (60 ml/2 fl oz) boiling water

2 eggs

½ cup (125 ml/4 fl oz) light oil (e.g. sunflower, rice bran, canola, light olive oil) or melted butter

1 cup (250 ml/9 fl oz) full-cream milk (or non-dairy alternative)

1⅔ cups (275 g/9¾ oz) gluten-free self-raising flour (see page 15 for recipe)

¼ teaspoon bicarbonate of soda (baking soda), sifted

1 teaspoon salt

½ teaspoon cracked black pepper

½ teaspoon ground nutmeg

½ cup (70 g/2½ oz) finely grated zucchini (courgette)

½ cup (70 g/2½ oz) cubed feta, plus extra to garnish

1 teaspoon finely chopped rosemary leaves, plus a little extra to garnish

Preheat the oven to 190°C/375°F (170°C/325°F fan-forced) with the oven rack positioned in the middle of the oven.

Toss the sweet potato in the olive oil and lightly roast on a baking tray lined with baking paper for 20 minutes. Remove from the oven and set aside to cool.

Line a large 6-hole muffin tin with high-sided muffin wraps (or grease the tin with a little butter or oil if not using papers).

Mix the chia seeds and boiling water together in a small bowl. Set aside for 2–3 minutes to form a gel.

Whisk the eggs, oil and milk together in a separate bowl. Tip in the chia gel and whisk again to break up the gel. Set aside.

Add the dry ingredients to a large bowl and whisk well to combine.

Using a spatula, tip the wet mix into the dry mix and gently fold it through until just combined. (The mix should still be lumpy.) Add half the roasted sweet potato, together with the zucchini, feta and rosemary and gently fold in until just mixed.

Using a ¼ cup spring-loaded ice-cream scoop, take a flat scoop and empty it into a muffin tin. Repeat the process so you have two scoops per muffin wrap. (The mix should be about two-thirds of the way up each muffin wrap, leaving enough room for the muffins to rise.)

Garnish the top of each muffin with a couple of pieces of roasted sweet potato, a few feta cubes and a little finely chopped rosemary. Transfer to the oven and bake for approximately 20 minutes. Rotate the tray and continue to bake for a further 10 minutes, or until the muffins are lightly golden and a skewer inserted into the centre of each comes out clean.

Remove the muffins from the oven and leave to cool in the tin for 5 minutes before turning out onto a wire rack. Serve warm or at room temperature.

STORAGE

These muffins will keep stored in an airtight container in the refrigerator for up to 3 days, or in the freezer for up to 1 month.

TIPS

- Fresh rosemary in muffins is always preferable to dried as it's more floral and less pungent. Don't be too generous with it, as it has quite a strong flavour.
- Roasted pumpkin makes a great replacement for the sweet potato, while ricotta and parmesan both work very well in place of the feta.

Roast Sweet Potato, Zucchini, Feta and Rosemary Muffins (page 141), Bacon, Cheddar, Cherry Tomato and Chive Muffins (page 145), Zucchini, Caramelised Onion, Parmesan and Thyme Muffins (page 140)

Bacon, Cheddar, Cherry Tomato and Chive Muffins

MAKES 6 LARGE MUFFINS

These muffins are wonderfully tasty, but a note about the tomatoes – I highly recommend using cherry tomatoes because the larger varieties have too much liquid in them, making the muffins a little soggy.

1 tablespoon chia seeds

¼ cup (60 ml/2 fl oz) boiling water

2 eggs

½ cup (125 ml/4 fl oz) light oil (e.g. sunflower, rice bran, canola, light olive oil) or melted butter

1 cup (250 ml/9 fl oz) full-cream milk (or non-dairy alternative)

1⅔ cups (275 g/9¾ oz) gluten-free self-raising flour (see page 15 for recipe)

1 tablespoon gluten-free baking powder

¼ teaspoon bicarbonate of soda (baking soda), sifted

1 teaspoon salt

½ teaspoon cracked black pepper

¾ cup (110 g/3¾ oz) chopped bacon

½ cup (50 g/1¾ oz) grated cheddar, plus extra to garnish

½ cup (70 g/2½ oz) cherry tomatoes, quartered, plus extra to garnish

½ bunch fresh chives, chopped, plus extra to garnish

Preheat the oven to 190°C/375°F (170°C/325°F fan-forced) with the oven rack positioned in the middle of the oven.

Line a large 6-hole muffin tin with high-sided muffin wraps (or grease the tin with a little butter or oil if not using papers).

Mix the chia seeds and boiling water together in a small bowl. Set aside for 2–3 minutes to form a gel.

Whisk the eggs, oil and milk together in a separate bowl. Tip in the chia gel and whisk again to break up the gel. Set aside.

Add the dry ingredients to a large bowl and whisk well to combine.

Using a spatula, tip the wet mix into the dry mix and gently fold it through until just mixed. (The mix should still be lumpy.) Add two-thirds of the bacon, and the cheddar, tomatoes and chives and gently fold in until just mixed.

Using a ¼ cup spring-loaded ice-cream scoop, take a flat scoop of mix and empty it into a muffin tin. Repeat the process so you have two scoops per muffin wrap. (The mix should be about two-thirds of the way up each muffin wrap, leaving room for the muffins to rise.)

Garnish the top of each muffin with a few extra bacon pieces, a little cheddar, some tomato quarters and a sprinkling of chives, then transfer to the oven and bake for approximately 20 minutes. Rotate the tray and continue to bake for a further 8–10 minutes, or until the muffins are lightly golden and a skewer inserted into the centre of each comes out clean.

Remove the muffins from the oven and leave to cool in the tin for 5 minutes before turning out onto a wire rack. Serve warm or at room temperature.

STORAGE

These muffins will keep stored in an airtight container in the refrigerator for up to 3 days, or in the freezer for up to 1 month.

TIPS

- Using a spring-loaded ice-cream scoop is definitely the cleanest way to scoop muffin mix and ensures even-sized muffins. I use a no. 16 scoop with a ¼ cup capacity.
- Removing the muffins from their tin to cool completely prevents them from sweating and going soggy.

SCONES
and PANCAKES

Though sweet often wins the day in our house, there
are times when only a savoury scone or pancake will do.
With soup or salad in place of a roll, the scones here
are sure to delight, while the corn pancakes are
a breakfast worth getting up for.

148–159

Fresh Herb Scones

MAKES 6 LARGE SCONES

These are my minimalist savoury scones, where herbs are the hero. Simple but so good. Enjoy warm with a little butter or as an accompaniment to soup or a salad.

2 cups (330 g/11½ oz) gluten-free self-raising flour (see page 15 for recipe), plus extra for dusting

1 teaspoon gluten-free baking powder

1½ teaspoons xanthan gum

¾ teaspoon bicarbonate of soda (baking soda)

1 teaspoon salt

½ teaspoon cracked black pepper

60 g (2¼ oz) cold unsalted butter, cut into small cubes (or non-dairy alternative)

1 egg, at room temperature

1 cup (250 ml/9 fl oz) buttermilk (or 200 ml/7 fl oz non-dairy milk mixed with 2 tablespoons lemon juice)

2 teaspoons fresh thyme leaves

1 large rosemary sprig, leaves picked and finely chopped

2 teaspoons finely chopped oregano leaves

2 teaspoons finely chopped flat-leaf parsley leaves

Preheat the oven to 170°C/325°F (150°C/300°F fan-forced) with the oven rack positioned in the middle of the oven.

Line a baking tray with baking paper.

Sift all the dry ingredients into a large bowl and whisk well to combine.

Rub in the butter using your fingers until the mixture resembles fine breadcrumbs. (It should not be lumpy – if it is, keep rubbing until there are no lumps.)

Add the egg and stir it into the mixture with a dessert spoon, then gently stir in half the buttermilk until just mixed in. Add the fresh herbs and remaining buttermilk and stir to form a moist dough.

Turn the dough onto a lightly floured surface and knead very gently to form a disc approximately 4 cm (1½ in) thick. Lightly flour the top of the dough.

Dip a 6 cm (2½ in) circular cutter in flour, then use it to cut out your scones – bringing the dough back together, re-flouring it and flattening it to get it back to the desired thickness as necessary. Transfer the scones to the lined baking tray, spacing them evenly.

Bake for 25–30 minutes, rotating the tray halfway through for even cooking, until lightly golden brown on top. Remove from the oven, transfer to a wire rack and leave to cool slightly. Serve warm with a little butter or non-dairy spread.

TIPS

- Using cold butter will make it easier to rub it into the flour without sticking to your fingers. A non-dairy alternative will be softer and a little trickier to work with, but the end result will be the same.
- Dusting the top of the dough and the cutter with flour will make it easier to cut out the scones.

STORAGE
These scones will keep stored in an airtight container for 3 days, or in the freezer for up to 1 month.

Cheddar, Corn and Chive Scones

MAKES 7 LARGE SCONES

I must make a batch of these at home once a month at least. My kids love them in their lunchbox or after school. While you can use fresh or frozen corn kernels here, I'd go for fresh where you can, as they're sweeter and more flavoursome and have a slight crunch.

2 cups (330 g/11½ oz) gluten-free self-raising flour (see page 15 for recipe), plus extra for dusting

1 teaspoon gluten-free baking powder

1½ teaspoons xanthan gum

¾ teaspoon bicarbonate of soda (baking soda)

1 teaspoon salt

½ teaspoon cracked black pepper

60 g (2¼ oz) cold unsalted butter, cut into small cubes (or non-dairy alternative)

1 egg, at room temperature

1 cup (250 ml/9 fl oz) buttermilk (or 200 ml/7 fl oz non-dairy milk mixed with 2 tablespoons lemon juice)

1½ cups (300 g/10½ oz) corn kernels (fresh or frozen and thawed)

1 cup (100 g/3½ oz) grated cheddar cheese (or non-dairy hard cheese)

½ bunch fresh chives, finely chopped

Preheat the oven to 170°C/325°F (150°C/300°F fan-forced) with the oven rack positioned in the middle of the oven.

Line a baking tray with baking paper.

Sift all the dry ingredients into a large bowl and whisk well to combine.

Rub in the butter using your fingers until the mixture resembles fine breadcrumbs. (It should not be lumpy – if it is, keep rubbing until there are no lumps.)

Add the egg and stir it into the mixture with a dessert spoon to combine, then gently stir in half the buttermilk until just mixed in. Add the corn, cheese, chives and remaining buttermilk and stir to form a moist dough.

Turn the dough onto a lightly floured surface and knead very gently to form a disc approximately 4 cm (1½ in) thick. Lightly flour the top of the dough.

Dip a 6 cm (2½ in) circular cutter in flour, then use it to cut out your scones – bringing the dough back together, re-flouring it and flattening it to get it back to the desired thickness as necessary. Transfer the scones to the lined baking tray, spacing them evenly.

Bake for 25–30 minutes, rotating the tray halfway through for even cooking, until lightly golden brown on top. Remove from the oven and leave to cool slightly. Serve warm with a little butter or non-dairy spread.

TIPS
- The secret to avoiding rock-hard scones is all in the handling. Kneading scone dough is a very quick process. It's important not to overwork the dough – the less you touch it, the better.
- Lining the tray with baking paper ensures the scones don't stick to the tray and will make them easier to move around, if necessary.

STORAGE
These scones will keep stored in an airtight container for 3 days, or in the freezer for up to 1 month.

Bacon, Cherry Tomato and Basil Scones

MAKES 7 LARGE SCONES

I love the combination of bacon and tomato in this scone, together with what is perhaps the most widely used herb in cooking, basil.

2 cups (330 g/11½ oz) gluten-free self-raising flour (see page 15 for recipe), plus extra for dusting

1½ teaspoons xanthan gum

¾ teaspoon bicarbonate of soda (baking soda)

1 teaspoon gluten-free baking powder

1 teaspoon salt

½ teaspoon cracked black pepper

60 g (2¼ oz) cold unsalted butter, cut into small cubes (or non-dairy alternative)

1 egg, at room temperature

1 cup (250 ml/9 fl oz) buttermilk (or 200 ml/7 fl oz non-dairy milk mixed with 2 tablespoons lemon juice)

1 cup (150 g/5½ oz) finely chopped bacon

½ cup (70 g/2½ oz) cherry tomatoes, cut into eighths

10 fresh basil leaves, finely shredded

STORAGE

These scones will keep stored in an airtight container for up to 3 days, or in the freezer for up to 1 month.

Preheat the oven to 200°C/400°F (180°C/350°F fan-forced) with the oven rack positioned in the middle of the oven.

Line a baking tray with baking paper.

Sift all the dry ingredients into a large bowl and whisk well to combine.

Add the butter (or any non-dairy spread) and, using your fingers, rub it into the flour mixture until the mixture resembles fine breadcrumbs. (It should not be lumpy – if it is, keep rubbing until there are no lumps.)

Add the egg and stir it into the mixture with a spoon to combine, then gently stir in half of the buttermilk until just mixed in. Add the bacon, cherry tomatoes and basil and repeat the process with the remaining buttermilk to form a moist dough.

Turn the dough onto a lightly floured surface and knead very gently to form a disc approximately 5 cm (2 in) thick. Lightly flour the top of the dough.

Dip a 6 cm (2½ in) circular cutter in flour, then use it to cut out your scones – bringing the dough back together, re-flouring it and flattening it to get it back to the desired thickness as necessary. Transfer the scones to the lined baking tray, spacing them out evenly.

Bake the scones for 25–30 minutes, rotating the tray halfway through for even cooking, until lightly golden brown on top. Remove from the oven and leave to cool slightly. Serve warm with a little butter or non-dairy spread.

TIPS

- Keeping your scone discs thick like this will ensure they have plenty of height once baked.
- Always finely shred basil leaves that are stacked on top of each other. Chopping basil simply bruises the leaves and turns it black.
- Using cherry tomatoes is less wet than using regular tomatoes, which will give you a soggy dough that's more difficult to work with.

Cheddar, Corn and Chive Scones (page 152),
Bacon, Cherry Tomato and Basil Scones (page 153)

Roast Pumpkin, Parmesan and Thyme Scones

MAKES 7 LARGE SCONES

These lovely savoury scones require the same deft handling as sweet scones to ensure a successful outcome (wonderfully light, flaky and well rounded, as opposed to depressingly hard, dense and flat). My big tip? Read the recipe through before you get cracking, and follow it to the letter.

300 g (10½ oz) pumpkin, peeled and chopped into chunky bite-sized pieces

2 teaspoons olive oil

2 cups (330 g/11½ oz) gluten-free self-raising flour (see page 15 for recipe), plus extra for dusting

1 teaspoon gluten-free baking powder

1½ teaspoons xanthan gum

¾ teaspoon bicarbonate of soda (baking soda)

1 teaspoon salt

½ teaspoon cracked black pepper

60 g (2¼ oz) cold unsalted butter, cut into small cubes (or non-dairy alternative)

1 egg, at room temperature

1 cup (250 ml/9 fl oz) buttermilk (or 200 ml/7 fl oz non-dairy milk mixed with 2 tablespoons lemon juice)

½ cup (50 g/1¾ oz) grated parmesan

½ bunch fresh thyme leaves, finely chopped

STORAGE

These scones will keep stored in an airtight container for 3 days, or in the freezer for up to 1 month.

Preheat the oven to 170°C/325°F (150°C/300°F fan-forced) with the oven rack positioned in the middle of the oven. Line a baking tray with baking paper.

Toss the pumpkin in a bowl with the oil. Arrange the pumpkin pieces on a lined baking tray and bake for 15–20 minutes, until just cooked. Remove from the oven and set aside to cool.

Line a baking tray with baking paper.

Sift all the dry ingredients into a large bowl and whisk well to combine.

Rub in the butter using your fingers until the mixture resembles fine breadcrumbs. (It should not be lumpy – if it is, keep rubbing until there are no lumps.)

Add the egg and stir it into the mixture with a dessert spoon to combine, then gently stir in half of the buttermilk until just mixed in. Add the pumpkin, parmesan, thyme and remaining buttermilk and stir to form a moist dough. (Be sure to fold the ingredients through gently so as not to break the pumpkin up too much.)

Turn the dough onto a lightly floured surface and knead very gently to form a disc approximately 4 cm (1½ in) thick. Lightly flour the top of the dough.

Dip a 6 cm (2½ in) circular cutter in flour, then use it to cut out your scones – bringing the dough back together, re-flouring it and flattening it to get it back to the desired thickness as necessary. Transfer the scones to the lined baking tray, spacing them evenly.

Bake for 25–30 minutes, rotating the tray halfway through for even cooking, until lightly golden brown on top. Remove from the oven and leave to cool slightly. Serve warm with a little butter or non-dairy spread.

TIP

- These scones are forgiving when it comes to changing the flavours: try replacing the pumpkin with cherry tomatoes or roasted sweet potato, the thyme with half a bunch of fresh basil or a quarter of a bunch of rosemary, and the parmesan with feta or cheddar.

Corn, Green Chilli and Coriander Buttermilk Pancakes

MAKES APPROXIMATELY 12 PANCAKES

I'm usually flexible and happy for you to substitute ingredients. But when it comes to replacing fresh herbs with dried in this recipe, I have to say… don't do it! You'll be so much happier with the result if you can rustle up the fresh stuff, believe me.

1 cup (165 g/5¾ oz) gluten-free self-raising flour (see page 15 for recipe)

¼ teaspoon bicarbonate of soda (baking soda)

½ teaspoon salt

¼ teaspoon cracked black pepper

2 eggs

350 ml (12 fl oz) buttermilk (or 250 ml/9 fl oz) non-dairy milk mixed with 1 tablespoon lemon juice)

25 g (1 oz) unsalted butter (or non-dairy alternative), melted, plus extra for cooking

1½ cups (300 g/10½ oz) corn kernels, fresh or frozen and thawed

1 large spring onion (scallion), thinly sliced

1 large green chilli, finely chopped

¼ bunch fresh coriander (cilantro), leaves picked and chopped

STORAGE

Cooked pancakes are best eaten on the day but can be stored in the fridge for up to 1 day. Just reheat and serve.

Sift all the dry ingredients together into a large bowl and whisk to combine.

Whisk the eggs and buttermilk together in a separate bowl.

Add the melted butter to the egg mix and whisk again.

Pour the wet mix into the dry mix and whisk until smooth. Fold in the corn, spring onion, chilli and coriander.

Melt a little extra butter in a non-stick frying pan over low–medium heat, tilting the pan to make sure the base is evenly coated.

Using a ladle or a serving spoon, drop approximately ⅓ cup (80 ml/2½ fl oz) mix into the centre of the pan, smoothing it out with the back of your spoon and shaping it into a rough circle approximately 12 cm (4½ in) in diameter.

Cook for 2 minutes, or until bubbles appear on the surface of the pancake and the underside is evenly golden (use your spatula to check), then flip it over and cook for a further 2 minutes, until evenly golden on both sides.

Slide the cooked pancake onto a plate and repeat the process until all the pancake mix has been used, adding more butter to the pan between pancakes as needed. Serve with bacon and maple syrup (opposite) or chopped tomato, avocado, mixed leaves and a little relish or onion jam.

TIPS
- The pancake batter can be made up to 1 day ahead and kept in the fridge until needed. Mix before using.
- The buttermilk helps to create light and fluffy pancakes. If you are using a milk substitute combined with lemon juice, you'll need to use less, otherwise the mix will be too runny.
- While you can use fresh or frozen corn kernels here, fresh definitely gives the pancakes a little bit of crunch and more flavour, which I love! To turn down the heat levels, omit the seeds when chopping the chilli.

PASTRY, QUICHES and PIES

Whether it's a creamy, delicate quiche or a hearty,
slow-cooked meat pie, this is where savoury baking shines
brightest. As with all recipes involving pastry, I turn to
these when I have a bit more time and attention to bring
to the process. The results are always worth it.

160—181

Savoury Decadent Shortcrust Pastry

MAKES 1 KG (2 LB 4 OZ)

It's taken me a long time to crack the code for making a great gluten-free pastry: short but not too crumbly, and, of course, great-tasting. You can use this recipe to make any savoury pastry, including pies, quiches and sausage rolls.

2⅔ cups (440 g/15½ oz) gluten-free plain (all-purpose) flour (see page 15 for recipe)

2½ teaspoons xanthan gum

1 teaspoon salt

280 g (10 oz) cold unsalted butter, cut into small cubes

⅓ cup (85 g/3 oz) sour cream

1 large egg, at room temperature

STORAGE

Uncooked pastry dough can be kept refrigerated for up to 1 week or frozen for up to 1 month. Any excess unused dough should be flattened to no more than 3 cm (1¼ in) thick and wrapped well in plastic wrap for later use. If frozen, simply defrost in the refrigerator and use while cold.

Add the flour, xanthan gum and salt to a food processor and whiz together for 10 seconds. Add the butter and mix for 30 seconds, until the mixture resembles breadcrumbs, then add the sour cream and egg and mix for 10 seconds, until it comes together and forms a ball.

Turn the soft dough out onto a sheet of plastic wrap and wrap well, flattening the dough to a disc approximately 2 cm (¾ in) thick. Rest the dough by chilling in the fridge for at least 1 hour, ideally overnight. (This will make it easier to work with – day-old pastry always works best!)

Once rested, unwrap the dough, transfer it to a floured surface and leave it for 2–3 minutes to soften. Using a floured rolling pin, work the dough by rolling it out, folding it back on itself and then rolling it out again. Repeat this process a few times over, then roll the pastry out to a 2 cm (¾ in) thickness, rewrap and chill until needed.

When you're ready to use the dough, unwrap it and leave it on a lightly floured bench for 2–3 minutes to warm up. Once the pastry has softened slightly, rub a little flour over the surface.

Using a lightly floured rolling pin, roll the pastry out as required, rolling a few times one way, then flipping it over and re-flouring the bench and rolling pin as necessary. (The trick here is not to over-flour the pastry, as this will dry it out – just add as much as you need so the dough is workable.)

Now the pastry is ready for cutting out and/or lining. When using a cutter, make sure it is lightly floured, so it doesn't stick to the pastry. When lining, grease the tart ring or pie tin/dish with butter or a spray oil and place on a tray lined with baking paper. Always cut the pastry so it's oversized before you line it, then gently let the pastry fall into the tin/dish – this way, you can cut the excess pastry once you've finished and have less shrinkage when baking. Don't stretch the pastry, as it will become too thin and fall apart.

If the pastry is going to be filled then baked, there is no need to parbake it first. If you are planning on finishing it with fresh ingredients, then bake at 180–190°C/350–375°F (160–170°C/315–325°F fan-forced) until golden. Remove from the oven and leave to cool completely before filling.

Savoury Dairy-free Shortcrust Pastry

MAKES 1 KG (2 LB 4 OZ)

If dairy-free is your preference, you'll love this recipe. You just need to work fast to keep the margarine cold and make the dough easier to handle.

2⅔ cups (440 g/15½ oz) gluten-free plain (all-purpose) flour (see page 15 for recipe)

2½ teaspoons xanthan gum

1 teaspoon salt

415 g (14¾ oz) cold hard cooking dairy-free margarine, cut into small cubes

1 egg, lightly beaten

STORAGE

Uncooked pastry dough can be kept refrigerated for up to 1 week or frozen for up to 1 month. Any excess unused dough should be flattened to no more than 3 cm (1¼ in) thick and wrapped well in plastic wrap for later use. If frozen, simply defrost in the refrigerator and use while cold.

Add the flour, xanthan gum and salt to a food processor and whiz together for 10 seconds. Add the margarine and mix for 15 seconds, until the mixture resembles breadcrumbs, then add the egg and mix for 10 seconds, until it comes together and forms a ball.

Turn the soft, sticky dough out onto a sheet of plastic wrap and wrap well, flattening the dough to a disc approximately 2 cm (¾ in) thick. Rest the dough by chilling in the fridge for at least 1 hour, ideally overnight. (This will make it easier to work with – day-old pastry always works best!)

When you're ready to use the dough, unwrap it and leave it on a lightly floured bench for 2–3 minutes to warm up. Once the pastry has softened slightly, rub a little flour over the surface.

Using a floured rolling pin, work the dough by rolling it out, folding it back on itself and then rolling it out again. Repeat this process a few times over, re-flouring the bench and rolling pin as necessary, then roll it out to the required thickness. (The trick here is not to over-flour the pastry as this will dry it out – just add as much as you need so the dough is workable.)

Now the pastry is ready for cutting out and/or lining. When using a cutter, make sure it is lightly floured, so it doesn't stick to the pastry. When lining, grease the tart or pie tin/dish with margarine or a spray oil and always cut your pastry so it's oversized before you line it, then gently let the pastry fall into the tin/dish – this way, you can cut the excess pastry once you've finished and have less shrinkage when baking. Don't stretch the pastry, as it will become too thin and fall apart.

If the pastry is going to be filled then baked, there is no need to parbake it first. If you are planning on finishing it with fresh ingredients, then bake it at 180–190°C/350–375°F (160–170°C/315–325°F fan-forced) until golden. Remove from the oven and leave to cool completely before filling.

TIP

- Margarine can be tricky to work with, as it softens quickly. If the pastry becomes too soft while rolling, simply chill it again until it's cool enough to work with.

Bacon, Cheddar, Onion and Thyme Quiche

SERVES 6-8

Bacon brings the umami, cheese the creaminess. Then there's onion for that sweet–savoury depth and thyme for the earthiness. In a word, moreish.

1 tablespoon olive oil

1¾ cups (260 g/9¼ oz) finely chopped bacon

1 onion, finely chopped

500 g (1 lb 2 oz) Savoury Decadent Shortcrust Pastry (see page 162)

1 cup (100 g/3½ oz) grated cheddar cheese

½ bunch thyme, leaves picked

salt and cracked black pepper

6 large eggs

1¼ cups (310 ml/10¾ fl oz) single (pure) cream

STORAGE

The cooked quiche can be stored in the refrigerator for up to 3 days or frozen in an airtight container for up to 1 month. Simply defrost and warm.

Preheat the oven to 190°C/375°F (170°C/325°F fan-forced) with the oven rack positioned in the middle of the oven.

Heat the oil in a non-stick frying pan. Add the bacon and sauté for 2 minutes. Add the onion and sauté for a further 2–3 minutes until lightly golden. Remove from the heat and set aside to cool.

Line a baking tray with baking paper.

Remove the base from a 26 x 4 cm (10 x 1½ in) loose-bottomed quiche tin and place the ring on the lined baking tray. Grease with a spray oil or butter.

Place the chilled and pre-worked pastry on a floured surface. Using a rolling pin, roll the pastry out into a 36 cm (14 in) disc approximately 5 mm (¼ in) thick. Gently place the pastry over the quiche ring and let it fall into the tin, allowing it to drape over the top edge. Lightly press the pastry into the shape of the tin and trim it at the top of the ring, leaving an excess 2 mm (⅛ in) or so above the top edge to allow for shrinkage while baking. (Any excess pastry can be rolled, flattened and refrigerated or frozen and used at another time.)

Scatter the cheddar over the base of the pastry, then top with the cooled bacon and onion mixture. Sprinkle the thyme leaves over and season with salt and pepper.

Whisk the eggs and cream together in a bowl and pour over the top, filling to 5 mm (¼ in) from the top.

Bake for 45–50 minutes, rotating the tray halfway through for even cooking, or until the centre of the filling feels firm to the touch and the pastry is golden underneath. (To check this, slide a spatula under the pastry and lift it slightly to take a look.) Once cooked, remove from the oven and leave to cool slightly on the tray.

When ready to serve, place an inverted plate over the quiche, flip it over and remove the ring, then place another inverted plate on the base of the quiche, flip it back over and remove the top plate. Slice and serve. Delicious with a fresh tomato salad.

TIP

- Excess pastry can be rerolled and refrigerated to use within a few days. Otherwise, if your pastry is fresh and hasn't yet been frozen, roll it out to a flattened disc, wrap completely in plastic and freeze for up to 1 month. Simply defrost at room temperature, roll and use while cold.

Cherry Tomato, Feta, Spanish Onion and Basil Quiche

SERVES 6–8

Quiches are incredibly forgiving – you can mix it up in terms of flavour as much as you like. But this combination of tomato and feta with onion and basil is a real winner.

500 g (1 lb 2 oz) Savoury Decadent Shortcrust Pastry (see page 162)

1½ cups (70 g/2½ oz) baby spinach leaves

1½ cups (220 g/7¾ oz) mixed cherry tomatoes

1 small red onion, thinly sliced

1 cup (130 g/4½ oz) crumbled feta

1 handful basil leaves, finely shredded

salt and cracked black pepper

6 large eggs

1¼ cups (310 ml/10¾ fl oz) single (pure) cream

STORAGE

The cooked quiche can be stored in the refrigerator for up to 3 days or frozen in an airtight container for up to 1 month. Simply defrost and warm in oven.

Preheat the oven to 190°C/375°F (170°C/325°F fan-forced) with the oven rack positioned in the middle of the oven.

Line a baking tray with baking paper.

Remove the base from a 26 x 4 cm (10½ x 1½ in) loose-bottomed quiche tin and place the ring on the lined baking tray. Grease with a spray oil or butter.

Place the chilled and pre-worked pastry on a floured surface. Using a rolling pin, roll the pastry out into a 36 cm (14 in) disc approximately 5 mm (¼ in) thick. Gently place the pastry over the quiche ring and let it fall into the tin, allowing it to drape over the top edge. Lightly press the pastry into the shape of the tin and trim it at the top of the ring, leaving an excess 2 mm (⅛ in) or so above the top edge to allow for shrinkage while baking. (Any excess pastry can be rolled, flattened and refrigerated or frozen and used at another time.)

Scatter the spinach leaves over the base, then top with the cherry tomatoes, onion and feta. Sprinkle the basil over and season with salt and pepper.

Whisk the eggs and cream together in a bowl and pour over the top, filling to 5 mm (¼ in) from the top.

Bake for 45–50 minutes, rotating the tray halfway through for even cooking, or until the centre of the filling feels firm to the touch and the pastry is golden underneath. (To check this, slide a spatula under the pastry and lift it slightly to take a look.) Once cooked, remove from the oven and leave to cool slightly on the tray.

When ready to serve, place an inverted plate over the quiche, flip it over and remove the ring, then place another inverted plate on the base of the quiche, flip it back over and remove the top plate. Enjoy with a mixed green salad.

TIP
- After pouring the egg and cream mix into the tin, move the mix gently around with a spoon so that it will combine properly with the filling and so that you can see more of the tomato, feta and spinach.

Hot-smoked salmon, Asparagus, Pea and Leek Quiche

SERVES 6–8

A few hero ingredients transform a humble quiche into a showstopper, both taste-wise as well as aesthetically: hot-smoked salmon provides pops of colour and flavour, and asparagus kept whole creates a beautiful pattern as well as being delicious.

1 leek, thinly sliced

1 tablespoon olive oil

500 g (1 lb 2 oz) Savoury Decadent Shortcrust Pastry (see page 162)

⅔ cup (90 g/3¼ oz) frozen peas

300 g (10½ oz) hot-smoked salmon, flaked

1 bunch asparagus, ends trimmed

1 handful dill leaves, roughly chopped

salt and cracked black pepper

6 large eggs

1¼ cups (310 ml/10¾ fl oz) single (pure) cream

STORAGE

The cooked quiche can be stored in the refrigerator for up to 3 days or frozen in an airtight container for up to 1 month. Simply defrost and warm.

Preheat the oven to 190°C/375°F (170°C/325°F fan-forced) with the oven rack positioned in the middle of the oven.

Line a baking tray with baking paper.

Remove the base from a 26 x 4 cm (10½ x 1½ in) loose-bottomed quiche tin and place the ring on the lined baking tray. Grease with a spray oil or butter.

In a frying pan, sauté the leek in a little oil until lightly golden. Remove from the heat and set aside to cool.

Place the chilled and pre-worked pastry on a floured surface. Using a rolling pin, roll the pastry out into a 36 cm (14 in) disc approximately 5 mm (¼ in) thick. Gently place the pastry over the quiche ring and let it fall into the tin, allowing it to drape over the top edge. Lightly press the pastry into the shape of the tin and trim it at the top of the ring, leaving an excess 2 mm (⅛ in) or so above the top edge to allow for shrinkage while baking. (Any excess pastry can be rolled, flattened and refrigerated or frozen and used at another time.)

Arrange the cooked leek evenly over the base of the pastry, then top with the peas, hot-smoked salmon and asparagus. Sprinkle the chopped dill over and season with salt and pepper.

Whisk the eggs and cream together in a bowl and pour over the top, filling to 5 mm (¼ in) from the top.

Bake for 45–50 minutes, rotating the tray halfway through for even cooking, or until the centre of the filling feels firm to the touch and the pastry is golden underneath. (To check this, slide a spatula under the pastry and lift it slightly to take a look.) Once cooked, remove from the oven and leave to cool slightly on the tray.

To serve, place an inverted plate over the quiche, flip it over and remove the ring, then place another inverted plate on the base of the quiche, flip it back over and remove the top plate. Slice and serve.

TIPS

- Keeping the asparagus whole lends the quiche a beautiful appearance. Try arranging it in different directions to create patterns.
- While hot-smoked salmon lends this quiche a lovely flavour, smoked salmon, or even freshly cooked salmon or trout, works well here too.

French Lentil, Spinach and Sweet Potato Pie

MAKES 6 INDIVIDUAL PIES

How to make a gluten-free vegetarian happy? Rustle up this delectable pie that combines a perfect mix of pulses, greens and warming sweet potato. Make the Savoury Decadent Shortcrust Pastry a day ahead if you can and chill it until needed.

1 kg (2 lb 4 oz) Savoury Decadent Shortcrust Pastry (see page 162)

1 large egg yolk, lightly beaten

FILLING

2 tablespoons olive oil

1 onion, finely chopped

4 garlic cloves, finely chopped

2 celery stalks, finely chopped

1 sweet potato (about 140 g/ 5 oz), cut into 1 cm (½ in) pieces

1 cup (210 g/7½ oz) puy lentils

½ teaspoon ground coriander

1 teaspoon ground cumin

3 thyme sprigs

1 bay leaf

1½ cups (375 ml/13 fl oz) tomato passata (puréed tomatoes)

3¾ cups (935 ml/32 fl oz) gluten-free vegetable stock or broth

1½ cups (70 g/2½ oz) baby spinach leaves

1 large handful coriander (cilantro) leaves, chopped

salt and cracked black pepper

STORAGE

Uncooked pies can be refrigerated for 1 day (glaze with egg yolk before baking). Cooked pies can be refrigerated for 3 days or frozen for up to 1 month.

For the filling, heat the olive oil in a frying pan over medium heat, add the onion, garlic and celery, and sauté for 2–3 minutes until soft. Add the sweet potato and lentils, and sauté for a further 2–3 minutes, then add the spices, thyme, bay leaf, passata and stock, reserving ¼ cup. Bring to the boil, reduce the heat to a simmer and cook for 15 minutes, then add the spinach and simmer for a further 5 minutes, or until almost all the liquid has been absorbed. Stir in the coriander leaves and season with salt and pepper to taste, then remove from the heat and set aside to cool completely.

Preheat the oven to 180°C/350°F (160°C/315°F fan-forced) with the oven rack positioned in the middle of the oven.

Grease six individual 12.5 cm (5 in) pie tins with butter or a spray oil. Place the chilled and pre-worked pastry on a floured surface. Using a rolling pin, roll it out to about 5 mm (¼ in) thick and cut into twelve 13.5 cm (5½ in) rounds.

Take a pastry round and let it gently fall into one of the tins, allowing the pastry to drape slightly over the top edge. Lightly press the pastry into the shape of the tin. Repeat with five more pastry rounds. Fill the pies to the top with the cooled filling, then take a pastry round, brush it with a little egg yolk around the outer edge and place it over a pie, egg-side down. Gently press the edges of the pastry together around the top of the pie to make sure they stay stuck together. Repeat this process for the remaining pies.

Using a skewer, make a small hole at least 2 mm (⅛ in) wide in the centre of each pie. Brush the tops with the beaten egg yolk.

Bake for 30 minutes, rotating the tray halfway through cooking, until golden.

Remove the pies from the oven and leave them to sit in their tins for 5 minutes to cool slightly. Delicious served with a mixed green salad.

TIPS

- Be careful not to stretch the pastry when rolling, as it will become too thin and fall apart.
- This can be made into a big family pie. Just cut the pastry to suit your pie tin/dish and bake for 10–15 minutes longer, until the top is golden.
- For really golden pies, brush them with egg yolk twice, chilling them for at least 20 minutes after the first brushing so the egg dries between applications.

Barramundi, Potato and Fennel Pie

MAKES 1 FAMILY PIE

Fish pies are back in vogue of late. And for good reason – they're so nourishing and they taste great. I've chosen barramundi here because of its firm texture and slightly sweet, subtle taste, but other firm fish will work too. Kids will love it!

1 kg (2 lb 4 oz) Savoury Decadent Shortcrust Pastry (see page 162)

1 large egg yolk, lightly beaten

FILLING

400 g (14 oz) small waxy potatoes

2 tablespoons butter

1 leek, white end only, thinly sliced

1 small fennel bulb, thinly sliced

4 garlic cloves, finely chopped

1 tablespoon finely chopped capers

½ cup (75 g/2½ oz) frozen peas

½ cup (125 ml/4 fl oz) gluten-free fish stock

½ cup (125 ml/4 fl oz) single (pure) cream

500 g (1 lb 2 oz) barramundi fillet, skin off, cut into bite-sized chunks

1 small bunch dill, finely chopped

salt and cracked black pepper

STORAGE

Uncooked pies can be refrigerated for 1 day (glaze with egg yolk before baking). Cooked pies can be refrigerated for 3 days or frozen for up to 1 month.

For the filling, place the potatoes in a stockpot or large saucepan and cover with water. Bring to the boil on high heat then reduce the heat to medium and cook for 15–20 minutes, or until just cooked. (Check with a fork for tenderness – the potatoes should be still firm, not falling apart.)

Once cooked, drain the potatoes and leave to cool, then peel with a paring knife and cut into bite-sized pieces. Set aside.

Melt the butter in a large frying pan over medium heat. Add the leek and fennel and sauté for 8–10 minutes, until softened, then add the garlic, capers and peas and sauté for a further 2–3 minutes.

Pour in the stock and cream and bring to a gentle boil, then reduce the heat and simmer for 2–3 minutes to thicken slightly. Add the potatoes, fish and dill, season to taste with salt and pepper and simmer for a further 1 minute, stirring, until everything is coated in the creamy sauce. Remove from the heat, spoon into a large airtight container and transfer to the refrigerator to cool.

Preheat the oven to 180°C/350°F (160°C/315°F fan-forced) with the oven rack positioned in the middle of the oven.

Grease a 30 x 20 cm (12 x 8 in) pie tin with butter or a spray oil. Place the chilled and pre-worked pastry on a floured surface. Divide the dough in half and using a rolling pin, roll each half out into a rectangle approximately 5 mm (¼ in) thick and a little larger than the dimensions of your tin.

To make the pie, take one of the pastry rectangles and let it gently fall into the tin, allowing the pastry to drape slightly over the top edge. Lightly press the pastry into the shape of the tin. Fill the pie to the top with the cooled filling, then take the remaining pastry rectangle, brush it with a little egg yolk around the outer edges and place it over the pie, egg-side down. Gently press the edges of the pastry together around the top of the pie to make sure they stay stuck together.

Using a skewer, make a small hole at least 2 mm (⅛ in) wide in the centre of the pie. Brush the top with the beaten egg yolk.

Bake for 30 minutes, rotating the tray halfway through cooking, until golden.

Remove the pie from the oven and leave to sit in the tin for 5 minutes to cool slightly. Delicious served with a salad of shaved radish and mixed green leaves.

Barramundi, Potato and Fennel Pie (page 173),
French Lentil, Spinach and Sweet Potato Pie
(page 172)

Chicken, Leek, Pea and Tarragon Pie

SERVES 8

Chicken pies are real crowd-pleasers. This one is particularly scrumptious thanks to the leek, which gives the pie a little sweetness, and tarragon's subtle liquorice-like taste.

1 kg (2 lb 4 oz) Savoury Decadent Shortcrust Pastry (see page 162)

1 large egg yolk, lightly beaten

1 teaspoon water

1 tablespoon white sesame seeds

FILLING

1 kg (2 lb 4 oz) chicken thigh fillets, cut into 1cm (½ in) cubes

1 leek, trimmed and thinly sliced

4 garlic cloves, chopped

2¼ cups (560 ml/19¼ fl oz) gluten-free chicken stock or broth

2 cups (280 g/10 oz) fresh or frozen peas

2–3 tablespoons finely chopped tarragon leaves

2 tablespoons dijon mustard

1 cup (250 ml/9 fl oz) single (pure) cream

2 tablespoons gluten-free plain (all-purpose) flour (see page 15 for recipe)

salt and cracked black pepper

Make up the savoury decadent shortcrust pastry (preferably a day ahead) and chill until needed.

Preheat the oven to 180°C/350°F (160°C/315°F fan-forced) with the oven rack positioned in the middle of the oven.

For the filling, put the chicken thigh fillets, leek and garlic in a deep baking tray and pour over the chicken stock or broth. Cover the baking tray with foil and bake for 30–40 minutes, or until the chicken is just cooked through. Remove the tray from the oven and leave the chicken to cool for in the poaching liquid for 10 minutes or until cool enough to handle, then dice into small bite-sized pieces and place in a large bowl together with the leek, peas and tarragon. Strain the poaching liquid, measuring out 1 cup.

Transfer the strained, measured stock to a saucepan together with the dijon mustard and cream and warm, stirring, over medium heat. Once hot, sift the flour into the liquid and whisk until simmering and thickened to a sauce-like consistency.

Tip the sauce over your chicken mix and gently stir to combine. Season with plenty of salt and pepper to taste, then transfer to the refrigerator to cool.

Adjust the oven temperature to 190°C/375°F (170°C/325°F fan-forced).

Grease a 24 x 4.5 cm (9½ x 1¾ in) circular pie tin with butter or a spray oil and line with baking paper.

Whisk the beaten egg yolk and water together in a small bowl. Set aside.

Place the chilled pre-worked pastry on a floured surface. Using a rolling pin, roll the pastry out into a 34 cm (13¼ in) disc approximately 4 mm (¼ in) thick. Gently place the pastry over the pie tin and let it fall into the tin, allowing it to drape over the top edge. Lightly press the pastry into the shape of the tin. Trim the excess pastry around the edge and roll it out into a roughly 24 cm (9½ in) x 3 mm (¼ in) disc large enough to cover the top of the pie.

Fill the pie to the top with the cooled filling.

The cooked pie can be refrigerated for up to 3 days or frozen for up to 1 month. If freezing the uncooked pie, don't sprinkle the sesame seeds on top until after the pie is defrosted, glazing it again with egg yolk and water and sprinkling them over when ready to bake instead.

Brush a little of the egg yolk and water mix around the outer edge of the pastry base, then place the pie top over the pie and press firmly around the edges.

Cut a small cross in the centre of the pie to allow it to vent while cooking, then gently brush the top with the egg yolk mix. Sprinkle the sesame seeds over.

Bake for 45–50 minutes, rotating the tray halfway through cooking, until golden.

Remove the pie from the oven and leave it to sit in the pie tin for at least 5 minutes to cool slightly. Delicious served with a salad of shaved fennel and mixed greens.

TIPS

- I like to use chicken thigh in my pies, as it's a tender cut that's more flavoursome than breast, which has a tendency to dry out when cooked like this.
- As leeks can be very dirty, be sure to wash them well before using (no one wants a gritty-tasting pie).

Chicken, Leek, Pea and Tarragon Pie (page 176)

Slow-cooked Beef and Mushroom Pies (page 180)

Slow-Cooked Beef and Mushroom Pies

MAKES 6 INDIVIDUAL PIES

Meat pies have been popular since Ancient Roman times. This one makes a hero of chuck beef, which becomes wonderfully tender and tasty after slow cooking, as well as mushrooms, spices and red wine. It's a firm favourite in our household.

1 kg (2 lb 4 oz) Savoury Decadent Shortcrust Pastry (see page 162)

1 large egg yolk, lightly beaten

FILLING

500 g (1 lb 2 oz) beef chuck, cut into 1 cm (½ in) cubes

¼ cup (40 g/1½ oz) gluten-free plain (all-purpose) flour (see page 15 for recipe)

⅓ cup (80 ml/2½ fl oz) olive oil

250 g (9 oz) mushrooms, sliced

2 tablespoons gluten-free worcestershire sauce

1 large onion, thinly sliced

4 garlic cloves, chopped

½ bunch fresh thyme, leaves picked

1½ cups (375 ml/13 fl oz) gluten-free beef stock or broth

⅔ cup (170 ml/5½ fl oz) medium-bodied red wine

2 tablespoons dijon mustard

salt and cracked black pepper

Preheat the oven to 180°C/350°F (160°C/315°F fan-forced) with the oven rack positioned in the middle of the oven.

For the filling, coat the beef in 2 tablespoons of the flour, shaking off the excess.

Heat 2 tablespoons of the olive oil in a non-stick frying pan over medium heat. Brown the meat in batches and transfer it to a large casserole dish.

In the same frying pan, heat 1 tablespoon of olive oil and cook the mushrooms in the worcestershire sauce for 5–7 minutes, until the sauce has evaporated and the mushrooms are lightly browned. Tip the cooked mushrooms into the casserole dish on top of the beef.

Add the remaining 1 tablespoon of olive oil to the pan together with the onion and sauté for 2–3 minutes until lightly browned. Add the garlic and sauté for a further 1 minute, then tip the mix into the casserole dish and add the thyme.

Add the stock or broth to the frying pan together with the red wine and mustard, stir well to deglaze the pan, and bring to a simmer. Pour this mixture over the beef and stir well. Cover the casserole dish with a lid or aluminium foil and bake for 1 hour, until the meat is tender and the flavours have melded.

Remove from the oven, take off the lid or foil and strain the liquid into a small saucepan. Sift the remaining 1 tablespoon of flour into the juices, then whisk over medium heat until the liquid thickens. Season to taste with salt and pepper.

Break the meat up slightly with a fork, then tip the thickened sauce over it and mix through. Tip the beef pie mix out into a large airtight container and cool in the refrigerator.

STORAGE

Any uncooked pies can be refrigerated for 1 day. Glaze with egg yolk before baking. Cooked pies can be refrigerated for 3 days or frozen for up to 1 month.

Grease six individual 12.5 cm (5 in) pie tins with butter or a spray oil. Place the chilled and pre-worked pastry on a floured surface. Using a rolling pin, roll it out to about 5 mm (¼ in) thick and cut into twelve 13.5 cm (5½ in) rounds.

Take a pastry round and let it fall gently into one of the tins, allowing the pastry to drape over the top edge. Lightly press the pastry into the shape of the tin. Repeat with five of the remaining pastry rounds. Fill the pies to the top with the cooled filling, then take a pastry round, brush it with a little egg yolk around the outer edge and place it over a pie, egg-side down. Gently press the edges of pastry together around the top to make sure they stay stuck together. Repeat this process for the remaining pies.

Using a skewer, make a small hole at least 2 mm (⅛ in) wide in the centre of each pie. Brush the tops with the beaten egg yolk.

Bake for 30 minutes, rotating the tray halfway through cooking, until golden.

Remove the pies from the oven and leave them to sit in their tins for 5 minutes to cool slightly. These are delicious served with bitter salad leaves such as radicchio to cut through the richness.

TIPS

- Chuck beef is a delicious cut when slow cooked for a long time, making it perfect for this recipe.
- Try not to omit the red wine as it adds depth of flavour to the filling.
- There is no need to clean the frying pan after cooking each batch of ingredients. Everything adds to the flavour.

PART *THREE*
bread

BRIOCHE and BUNS
184

FOCACCIA, FLATBREADS and LOAVES
202

BRIOCHE
and BUNS

I'm very pleased with the recipes here, as they have given a lot of people pleasure in gluten-free baking that they thought they might never have. From rich, buttery brioche to sweet, spice-laden or chocolate-filled hot cross buns, these are treats that no one should have to miss out on.

184–201

Brioche

MAKES 1 LOAF

Somewhere between a bread and a pastry sits this deliciously rich and almost buttery, yet light and airy, brioche. A quick heads-up that the batter is too sticky to handle, so you'll need to use a stand mixer or hand mixer.

1¼ cups (205 g/7¼ oz) gluten-free self-raising flour (see page 15 for recipe)

1½ cups (185 g/6½ oz) gluten-free cornflour (cornstarch)

½ teaspoon salt

3 teaspoons xanthan gum

1 teaspoon ground cinnamon

¼ cup (55 g/2 oz) caster (superfine) sugar

75 g (2½ oz) butter, melted, or 75 ml (2½ fl oz) light oil (e.g. sunflower, rice bran, canola, light olive oil)

2 tablespoons honey

300 ml (10½ fl oz) full-cream milk (or non-dairy alternative)

1 egg, at room temperature

1 tablespoon psyllium husk powder

½ cup (125 ml/4 fl oz) water

1½ teaspoons instant dried yeast

GLAZE

1 tablespoon milk

2 tablespoons raw sugar

STORAGE

Store at room temperature wrapped in plastic wrap or in an airtight container for up to 4 days. After day 1 the brioche will need to be toasted.

Preheat the oven to 190°C/375°F (170°C/325°F fan-forced) with the oven rack positioned in the lower half of the oven.

Grease a 23.5 x 10 x 10 cm (9¼ x 4 x 4 in) loaf tin and line the base and sides with baking paper.

Sift the dry ingredients except the psyllium husk powder and yeast into the bowl of a stand mixer and whisk to combine.

In a small saucepan, warm the butter and honey together, then remove from the heat and whisk in the milk and egg. Pour this mixture onto the sifted dry ingredients.

Using the dough hook attachment, mix on low for 1 minute to combine, then increase the speed to medium and mix for a further 8 minutes to work the xanthan gum into the batter. Stir the psyllium and water together to form a slurry, add to the bowl along with the yeast and mix for 1 minute more. (Alternatively, mix the ingredients together in a mixing bowl with a hand mixer.)

Leave the batter to sit for 5 minutes, then tip into the prepared loaf tin, smoothing and evening out the top with a spatula. Cover with oiled plastic wrap and leave to sit in a warm place for 30–40 minutes, or until the dough has risen to about 2 cm (¾ in) below the top of the tin (it will rise further during baking).

Remove the plastic wrap and use a pastry brush to very gently glaze the top of the brioche with the milk. Sprinkle the raw sugar over. Bake for 45 minutes, rotating the tin after the first 30 minutes for an even colour, until the crust is dark golden brown and firm to the touch all over.

Transfer the loaf to a wire rack and leave it to cool for 20 minutes before turning out to cool completely. Slice with a serrated knife and serve warm with butter.

TIPS
- Brioche that's 2–3 days old makes the best gluten-free breadcrumbs. Just trim the sugar crust off before whizzing pieces of brioche in a food processor to make the crumbs. Freeze for a longer shelf life.
- For individual brioches, before proving use a spring-loaded ice-cream scoop to transfer ½-cup scoops of batter onto a tray lined with baking paper. Prove on the tray, then glaze and bake for 25–30 minutes, until golden.

GLUTEN-FREE BAKING MADE SIMPLE

Fruit Brioche

MAKES 1 LOAF

The sultanas, orange zest and spices take this brioche to another level. Follow the recipe carefully and you'll be rewarded with a delicious lightly spiced fruit bread with a hint of orange.

1 cup (170 g/6 oz) sultanas

1¼ cups (205 g/7¼ oz) gluten-free self-raising flour (see page 15 for recipe)

1½ cups (185 g/6½ oz) gluten-free cornflour (cornstarch)

½ teaspoon salt

3 teaspoons xanthan gum

1 teaspoon ground cinnamon

½ teaspoon ground nutmeg

¼ cup (55 g/2 oz) caster (superfine) sugar

75 g (2½ oz) butter, melted, or 75 ml (2½ fl oz) light oil (e.g. sunflower, rice bran, canola, light olive oil)

2 tablespoons honey

300 ml (10½ fl oz) full-cream milk (or non-dairy alternative)

1 egg, at room temperature

1 tablespoon psyllium husk powder

½ cup (125 ml/4 fl oz) water

1½ teaspoons instant dried yeast

finely grated zest of 1 orange

GLAZE

1 tablespoon milk

2 tablespoons raw sugar

STORAGE

Store at room temperature in plastic wrap or in an airtight container for 3–4 days.

Place the sultanas in a small bowl and cover with boiling water. Leave to soak for 10 minutes, then drain and set aside.

Preheat the oven to 190°C/375°F (170°C/325°F fan-forced) with the oven rack positioned in the lower half of the oven.

Grease a 23.5 x 10 x 10 cm (9¼ x 4 x 4 in) loaf tin and line the base and sides with baking paper.

Sift the dry ingredients except the psyllium husk powder and yeast into the bowl of a stand mixer and whisk to combine.

In a small saucepan, warm the butter and honey together, then remove from the heat and whisk in the milk and egg. Pour this mixture onto the sifted dry ingredients.

Using the dough hook attachment, mix on low for 1 minute to combine, then increase the speed to medium and mix for a further 8 minutes to work the xanthan gum into the batter. Stir the psyllium and water together to form a slurry, add to the bowl along with the yeast, pre-soaked sultanas and orange zest and mix for 1 minute more. (Alternatively, mix the ingredients together in a mixing bowl with a hand mixer.)

Leave the batter to sit for 5 minutes, then tip into the prepared loaf tin, smoothing and evening out the top with a spatula. Cover with oiled plastic wrap and leave to sit in a warm place for 30–40 minutes, or until the dough has risen to about 2 cm (¾ in) below the top of the tin (it will rise further during baking).

Remove the plastic wrap and use a pastry brush to very gently glaze the top of the brioche with the milk. Sprinkle the raw sugar over. Bake for 45 minutes, rotating the loaf tin after the first 30 minutes for an even colour, until the crust is dark golden brown and firm to the touch all over.

Transfer the loaf to a wire rack and leave it to cool for 20 minutes before turning out to cool completely. Slice with a serrated knife and serve warm with butter.

TIPS

- Fruit brioche that's 2–3 days old makes the best French toast or bread and butter pudding.
- Pre-soaking the sultanas will soften them and help prevent them from drying out when baking.

Dark Chocolate Brioche

MAKES 1 LOAF

Spoil yourself at breakfast (or any time, really) with this fabulously rich, yet light and airy, chocolate brioche.

1¼ cups (205 g/7¼ oz) gluten-free self-raising flour (see page 15 for recipe)

1½ cups (185 g/6½ oz) gluten-free cornflour (cornstarch)

½ teaspoon salt

3 teaspoons xanthan gum

1 teaspoon ground cinnamon

¼ cup (55 g/2 oz) caster (superfine) sugar

75 g (2½ oz) butter, melted, or 75 ml (2½ fl oz) light oil (e.g. sunflower, rice bran, canola, light olive oil)

2 tablespoons honey

300 ml (10½ fl oz) full-cream milk (or non-dairy alternative)

1 egg, at room temperature

1 tablespoon psyllium husk powder

½ cup (125 ml/4 fl oz) water

1½ teaspoons instant dried yeast

1 cup (170 g/6 oz) dark chocolate chips

GLAZE

1 tablespoon milk

2 tablespoons raw sugar

STORAGE

Store at room temperature wrapped in plastic wrap or in an airtight container for up to 3–4 days. After day 1 the brioche will need to be toasted.

Preheat the oven to 190°C/375°F (170°C/325°F fan-forced) with the oven rack positioned in the middle of the oven.

Grease a 23.5 x 10 x 10 cm (9¼ x 4 x 4 in) loaf tin and line the base and sides with baking paper.

Sift the dry ingredients except the psyllium husk powder and yeast into the bowl of a stand mixer and whisk to combine.

In a small saucepan, warm the butter and honey together, then remove from the heat and whisk in the milk and egg. Pour this mixture onto the sifted dry ingredients.

Using the dough hook attachment, mix on low for 1 minute to combine, then increase the speed to medium and mix for a further 8 minutes to work the xanthan gum into the batter. Stir the psyllium and water together to form a slurry, add to the bowl along with the yeast and chocolate chips and mix for 1 minute more. (Alternatively, mix the ingredients together in a mixing bowl with a hand mixer.)

Leave the batter to sit for 5 minutes, then tip into the prepared loaf tin, smoothing and evening out the top with a spatula. Cover with oiled plastic wrap and leave to sit in a warm place for 30–40 minutes, or until the dough has risen to about 2 cm (¾ in) below the top of the tin (it will rise further during baking).

Remove the plastic wrap and use a pastry brush to very gently glaze the top of the brioche with the milk. Sprinkle the raw sugar over. Bake for 45 minutes, rotating the loaf tin after the first 30 minutes for an even colour, until the crust is dark golden brown and firm to the touch all over.

Transfer the loaf to a wire rack and leave it to cool for 20 minutes before turning out to cool completely. Slice with a serrated knife and serve warm with butter.

TIPS
- While you can replace the milk with non-dairy milk, I do prefer the texture and flavour that regular milk brings.
- I like to use a dark (54% cocoa solids) chocolate in this recipe, as it's richer and less sweet than milk chocolate.

Spinach and Feta Brioche

MAKES 1 LOAF

When you're craving a richer, more buttery version of bread, brioche hits the spot, especially when spinach and feta – one of life's great culinary marriages – are its hero ingredients.

1¼ cups (205 g/7¼ oz) gluten-free self-raising flour (see page 15 for recipe)

1½ cups (185 g/6½ oz) gluten-free cornflour (cornstarch)

½ teaspoon salt

3 teaspoons xanthan gum

1 teaspoon ground nutmeg

75 g (2½ oz) butter, melted, or 75 ml (2½ fl oz) light oil (e.g. sunflower, rice bran, canola, light olive oil)

¼ cup (60 ml/2 fl oz) rice syrup

300 ml (10½ fl oz) full-cream milk (or non-dairy alternative)

1 egg, at room temperature

1 tablespoon psyllium husk powder

½ cup (125 ml/4 fl oz) water

1½ teaspoons instant dried yeast

200 g (7 oz) frozen spinach, thawed and squeezed of excess liquid

½ cup (65 g/2¼ oz) feta, crumbled

½ cup (50 g/1¾ oz) coarsely grated parmesan, plus extra for garnish

½ bunch fresh dill, roughly chopped

1 tablespoon finely chopped mint leaves

Preheat the oven to 190°C/375°F (170°C/325°F fan-forced) with the oven rack positioned in the lower half of the oven.

Grease a 23.5 x 10 x 10 cm (9¼ x 4 x 4 in) loaf tin and line the base and sides with baking paper.

Sift the dry ingredients except the psyllium husk powder and yeast into the bowl of a stand mixer and whisk to combine.

In a small saucepan, warm the butter and rice syrup together, then remove from the heat and whisk in the milk and egg. Pour this mixture onto the sifted dry ingredients.

Using the dough hook attachment, mix on low for 1 minute to combine, then increase the speed to medium and mix for a further 8 minutes to work the xanthan gum into the batter. Stir the psyllium and water together to form a slurry, add to the bowl along with the yeast, spinach, cheeses and herbs and mix for 1 minute more. (Alternatively, mix the ingredients together in a mixing bowl with a hand mixer.)

Leave the batter to sit for 5 minutes, then tip into the prepared loaf tin, smoothing and evening out the top with a spatula. Cover with oiled plastic wrap and leave to sit in a warm place for 30–40 minutes, or until the dough has risen to about 2 cm (¾ in) below the top of the tin (it will rise further during baking).

Remove the plastic wrap and sprinkle the extra parmesan over. Bake for 45 minutes, rotating the loaf tin after the first 30 minutes for an even colour, until the crust is dark golden brown and firm to the touch all over.

Transfer the loaf to a wire rack and leave it to cool for 20 minutes before turning out to cool completely. Slice with a serrated knife and serve warm with butter.

TIPS

- If using oil, be sure to use a light-tasting one, as anything strong will influence the overall taste.
- Use fresh herbs rather than dried, as the latter will be too pungent.

STORAGE
Store this brioche in the refrigerator wrapped in plastic wrap for up to 3 days. After day 1 it will need to be toasted.

Fruit Hot Cross Buns

MAKES 16 BUNS

I've worked hard to make this recipe sing because I don't want anyone, whatever their religion, to miss out on one of life's simple but greatest pleasures – a hot cross bun with melted butter at Easter. Yum!

⅔ cup (120 g/4¼ oz) raisins

⅔ cup (120 g/4¼ oz) currants

1¼ cups (205 g/7¼ oz) gluten-free self-raising flour (see page 15 for recipe)

1½ cups (185 g/6½ oz) gluten-free cornflour (cornstarch)

½ cup (100 g/3½ oz) brown sugar,

½ teaspoon salt

3 teaspoons xanthan gum

2 teaspoons ground cinnamon

1 teaspoon ground nutmeg

⅓ teaspoon ground cloves

⅓ teaspoon ground cardamom

75 g (2½ oz) butter, melted, or 75 ml (2½ fl oz) light oil (e.g. sunflower, rice bran, canola, light olive oil)

1 large egg, at room temperature

1½ cups (375 ml/13 fl oz) full-cream milk (or non-dairy alternative), at room temperature

1 tablespoon psyllium husk powder

½ cup (125 ml/4 fl oz) water

1½ teaspoons instant dried yeast

zest of 1 orange

Place the raisins and currants in a small bowl and cover with boiling water. Leave to soak for 10–15 minutes, then drain and set aside.

Line a baking tray with baking paper.

Sift the dry ingredients except the psyllium husk powder and yeast into the bowl of a stand mixer and whisk to combine.

Whisk the butter, egg and milk together in a small bowl, then pour this mixture onto the sifted dry ingredients.

Using the dough hook attachment, mix on low for 1 minute to combine, then increase the speed to medium and mix for a further 8 minutes to work the xanthan gum into the batter. Stir the psyllium and water together to form a slurry, add to the bowl along with the yeast, pre-soaked raisins and currants and orange zest and mix for 1 minute more. (Alternatively, mix the ingredients together in a mixing bowl with a hand mixer.)

Leave the dough to rest in the bowl for 5 minutes. (This allows the psyllium to continue to absorb moisture and makes the dough a little easier to handle.)

Using a ⅓ cup spring-loaded ice-cream scoop for perfectly shaped buns, transfer slightly heaped scoops of batter onto the lined baking tray, keeping them 1 cm (½ in) apart.

Loosely cover the scooped buns with oiled plastic wrap and leave in a warm, draught-free spot to prove for approximately 30 minutes, or until risen by about a third.

Preheat the oven to 190°C/375°F (170°C/325°F fan-forced) with the oven rack positioned in the middle of the oven.

CROSS MIX (OPTIONAL)

⅔ cup (110 g/3¾ oz) gluten-free plain (all-purpose) flour (see page 15 for recipe)

¼ teaspoon ground nutmeg

⅔ cup (170 ml/5½ fl oz) water

2 teaspoons sunflower oil

SYRUP

½ cup (110 g/3¾ oz) white sugar

½ cup (125 ml/4 fl oz) water

finely grated zest of 1 orange

STORAGE

These buns will stay fresh in an airtight container at room temperature for 3–4 days or in the fridge for up to 5 days, but they will need to be toasted after the second day.

For the cross mix, if using, whisk the flour and nutmeg together in a bowl. Add the water and oil and whisk until smooth, then pour the batter into a piping bag fitted with a 7 mm (½ in) circular nozzle. (Alternatively, simply cut the end of the bag off where a nozzle would normally go so the opening is a similar size.)

Remove the plastic wrap from the buns. With a firm grip on the piping bag, pipe crosses on the buns, starting at one end of the tray and moving horizontally across each layer first and then vertically. Once done, place in the hot oven and bake for approximately 30 minutes, rotating the tray after the first 20 minutes for an even colour, until the buns are risen and golden and the tops spring back when you press down gently on them with two fingers.

While the buns are cooking, make the syrup. Bring the sugar and water to the boil in a small saucepan. Reduce the heat to low, add the orange zest and simmer for 5 minutes, or until reduced by a quarter.

Once the buns are cooked, remove them from the oven and brush all over with the hot glaze. Leave to sit for 10 minutes to absorb the glaze, then serve warm with butter.

TIPS

- Pre-soaking the raisins and currants will soften them and help prevent them drying out when baking.
- When making the cross mixture, be aware that flour blends can vary – you may need to add more or less water in order to find the right consistency.

*Hot Cross Buns (page 192), Chocolate Hot
Buns (page 196)*

Chocolate Hot Cross Buns

MAKES 16 BUNS

If you're vegan, you can make these buns using non-dairy milk and dairy-free chocolate. Either way they're delicious, and definitely best served warm so the chocolate melts slightly.

1¼ cups (205 g/7¼ oz) gluten-free self-raising flour (see page 15 for recipe)

1½ cups (185 g/6½ oz) gluten-free cornflour (cornstarch)

½ cup (100 g/3½ oz) brown sugar

½ teaspoon salt

3 teaspoons xanthan gum

2 teaspoons ground cinnamon

75 g (2½ oz) butter, melted, or 75 ml (2½ fl oz) light oil (e.g. sunflower, rice bran, canola, light olive oil)

1 large egg, at room temperature

1½ cups (375 ml/13 fl oz) full-cream milk (or non-dairy alternative), at room temperature

1 tablespoon psyllium husk powder

½ cup (125 ml/4 fl oz) water

1½ teaspoons instant dried yeast

1⅓ cups (220 g/7¾ oz) dark chocolate chips

Line a baking tray with baking paper.

Sift the dry ingredients except the psyllium husk powder and yeast into the bowl of a stand mixer and whisk to combine.

Whisk the butter, egg and milk together in a small bowl, then pour this mixture onto the sifted dry ingredients.

Using the dough hook attachment, mix on low for 1 minute to combine, then increase the speed to medium and mix for a further 8 minutes to work the xanthan gum into the batter. Stir the psyllium and water together to form a slurry, add to the bowl along with the yeast and chocolate and mix for 1 minute more. (Alternatively, mix the ingredients together in a mixing bowl with a hand mixer.)

Leave the dough to rest in the bowl for 5 minutes. (This allows the psyllium to continue to absorb moisture and makes the dough a little easier to handle.)

Using a ⅓ cup spring-loaded ice-cream scoop for perfectly shaped buns, transfer slightly heaped scoops of batter onto the lined baking tray, keeping them 1 cm (½ in) apart.

Loosely cover the scooped buns with oiled plastic wrap and leave in a warm, draught-free spot to prove for approximately 30 minutes, or until risen by about a third.

Preheat the oven to 190°C/375°F (170°C/325°F fan-forced) with the oven rack positioned in the middle of the oven.

CROSS MIX (OPTIONAL)

½ cup (85 g/3 oz) gluten-free plain (all-purpose) flour (see page 15 for recipe)

¼ cup (30 g/1 oz) cocoa powder

¼ teaspoon ground cinnamon

⅔ cup (170 ml/5½ fl oz) water

2 teaspoons sunflower oil

SYRUP

½ cup (110 g/3¾ oz) white (granulated) sugar

½ cup (125 ml/4 fl oz) water

STORAGE

These buns will stay fresh in an airtight container at room temperature for 3–4 days or in the fridge for up to 5 days, but they will need to be toasted after the second day.

For the cross mix, if using, sift the flour, cocoa powder and cinnamon together in a bowl. Add the water and oil and whisk together until smooth, then pour the batter into a piping bag fitted with a 7 mm (½ in) circular nozzle. (Alternatively, simply cut the end of the bag off where a nozzle would normally go so the opening is a similar size.)

Remove the plastic wrap from the buns. With a firm grip on the piping bag, pipe crosses on the buns, starting at one end of the tray and moving horizontally across each layer first and then vertically. Once done, place in the hot oven and bake for approximately 30 minutes, rotating the tray after the first 20 minutes for an even colour, until the buns are risen and golden and the tops spring back when you press down gently on them with two fingers.

While the buns are cooking, make the syrup. Bring the sugar and water to the boil in a small saucepan. Reduce the heat to low and simmer for 5 minutes, or until reduced by a quarter.

Once the buns are cooked, remove them from the oven and brush all over with the hot syrup. Leave to sit for 10 minutes to absorb the syrup, then serve warm with butter.

TIPS

- For a sweeter dough, replace the dark chocolate with milk chocolate (just make sure the chocolate pieces aren't too big so as not to affect the rise).
- Try adding orange zest to the syrup to give the buns a lovely jaffa flavour.

Cinnamon Pull-Apart Scrolls

MAKES 8 SCROLLS

I rarely offer guarantees in life but I'm making an exception with this recipe. It's incredibly easy, and I guarantee you'll end up with soft, fluffy and light cinnamon scrolls.

½ cup (100 g/3½ oz) brown sugar

1 tablespoon ground cinnamon

140 g (5 oz) butter, softened

1 batch of Buttermilk Scone Dough (see page 53 for recipe)

½ cup (125 ml/4 fl oz) single (pure) cream

ICING

¼ cup (60 g/2¼ oz) cream cheese

1 teaspoon vanilla extract

⅓ cup (40 g/1½ oz) gluten-free icing (confectioners') sugar

2 tablespoons milk or water

handful of chopped walnuts (optional)

STORAGE

These scrolls are best eaten on the day but can be stored in the refrigerator in an airtight container for up to 3 days. Reheat before serving.

Preheat the oven to 200°C/400°F (180°C/350°F fan-forced) with the oven rack positioned in the middle of the oven.

Grease 24 cm (9½ in) high-sided round cake tin and line the base and sides with baking paper.

Add the sugar, cinnamon and butter to a bowl and mix together to form a paste.

Roll the scone dough out on a floured surface into a 32 x 18 cm (13 x 7 in) rectangle, 1 cm (½ in) thick.

Spread the dough with the cinnamon butter to cover it evenly, then roll it up lengthways into a firm log. Using a floured serrated knife, cut the log at 4 cm (1½ in) intervals into eight equal-sized scrolls, then transfer to the prepared tin, tucking them in close to each other, with their prettiest cut sides facing up. Pour the cream over.

Bake for 45–50 minutes, until risen and golden and the top of the centre scroll springs back when you press down gently on it with two fingers.

Remove from the oven and leave to cool in the tin for 15–20 minutes.

While the scrolls are cooling, make the icing by whizzing the cream cheese, vanilla, icing sugar and milk together in a blender or food processor (or in a bowl with a hand mixer), until smooth, creamy and runny.

Tip the scrolls out onto a serving plate, drizzle all over with the icing and top with a handful of chopped walnuts, if you like. Serve immediately.

TIPS
- The buttermilk scone dough ensures the scrolls will be light and fluffy.
- To vary the icing, try melting chocolate and drizzling it over the scrolls.

Cheesy Garlic Pull-apart Buns

MAKES APPROXIMATELY 18 BUNS

Did this recipe have you at 'cheesy garlic'? It's a delicious combination that makes these buns completely moreish. Serve them up hot while the cheese is still wonderfully gooey.

1¼ cups (205 g/7¼ oz) gluten-free self-raising flour (see page 15 for recipe)

2 cups (250 g/9 oz) gluten-free cornflour (cornstarch)

2½ teaspoons salt, plus ½ teaspoon extra for sprinkling

1 teaspoon cracked black pepper

1 tablespoon xanthan gum

75 g (2½ oz) butter, melted, or 75 ml (2½ fl oz) light oil (e.g. sunflower, rice bran, canola, light olive oil)

1 large egg, at room temperature

1½ cups (375 ml/13 fl oz) full-cream milk (or non-dairy alternative)

1 tablespoon psyllium husk powder

½ cup (125 ml/4 fl oz) water

1½ teaspoons instant dried yeast

½ cup (50 g/1½ oz) coarsely grated parmesan

2 cups (250 g/9 oz) coarsely grated mozzarella cheese

6 large garlic cloves, crushed

⅓ bunch flat-leaf parsley leaves, finely chopped, plus extra to serve

STORAGE

These buns will keep in the fridge in an airtight container for up to 3 days. Reheat before eating.

Preheat the oven to 190°C/375°F (170°C/325°F fan-forced) with the oven rack positioned in the middle of the oven.

Grease a 22.5 x 33 x 6 cm (9 x 13 x 2½ in) baking dish and line it with baking paper.

Sift the dry ingredients except the psyllium husk powder and yeast into the bowl of a stand mixer and whisk to combine.

Whisk the butter, egg and milk together in a small bowl, then pour this mixture onto the sifted dry ingredients.

Using the dough hook attachment, mix on low for 1 minute to combine, then increase the speed to medium and mix for a further 8 minutes to work the xanthan gum into the batter. Stir the psyllium and water together to form a slurry, add to the bowl with the yeast, parmesan, half the mozzarella, the garlic and the parsley and mix for 1 minute more. (Alternatively, mix the ingredients together in a mixing bowl with a hand mixer.)

Leave the dough to sit for 5 minutes, then, using a ⅓ cup spring-loaded ice-cream scoop, transfer slightly heaped scoops of dough into the prepared dish, keeping them 1 cm (½ in) apart, starting in one corner and working your way across the dish, repeating until it is full and there is no more batter to scoop. Leave in a warm, draught-free spot to prove for 30 minutes, until risen by a third.

Once proved, scatter the extra salt and the remaining mozzarella cheese over the top, then transfer to the oven and bake for 40–45 minutes, until the buns are risen and golden, the cheese is well melted and the tops spring back when you press down gently on them with two fingers.

Remove from the oven and leave to cool slightly for 2 minutes. Serve hot while the cheese is melted and gooey, with a little extra chopped parsley scattered over the top.

TIPS

- The salt sprinkled on with the cheese really helps bring out the flavours, so don't be scared to add it. And feel free to use whichever cheeses you prefer – though try to stick to a combination of gooey and sharp flavour profiles.
- If you're not that keen on garlic, it's fine to leave it out.

FOCACCIA, FLATBREADS and LOAVES

If you've never tried gluten-free breadmaking before,
I urge you to give these recipes a go. Nothing here is hard
(the roti and naan are particularly easy) and the results
will make you wonder why you didn't do it sooner.

202–215

Bacon, Potato and Rosemary Focaccia

SERVES 8

Don't be daunted by focaccia. It's easier than you think to get a great fluffy result with a crisp yet chewy crust. This recipe harnesses the power of bacon and rosemary to give it a really yummy flavour.

2 cups (330 g/11½ oz) gluten-free plain (all-purpose) flour (see page 15 for recipe)

¾ teaspoon salt

¾ teaspoon gluten-free baking powder

2½ teaspoons instant dried yeast

1½ cups (375 ml/13 fl oz) buttermilk or water

2½ teaspoons rice syrup or raw caster (superfine) sugar

2 tablespoons olive oil, plus extra for sautéing and drizzling

250 g (9 oz) bacon rashers, rind removed and finely chopped

1 large potato, peeled and cut into 1.5 cm (½ in) cubes

3 large garlic cloves, cut into slivers

1–2 rosemary sprigs, leaves picked and chopped, plus extra to serve

sea salt flakes

STORAGE

The focaccia will keep in the refrigerator in an airtight container for up to 3 days. Reheat before serving.

Grease a 24 cm (9½ in) round cake tin or a 32 x 18 x 3 cm (13 x 7 x 1¼ in) brownie tray with olive oil.

Sift the dry ingredients into the bowl of a stand mixer with the paddle attachment fitted (or into a mixing bowl if using a hand mixer). Mix the dry ingredients on low speed for 10 seconds. Slowly add the buttermilk, rice syrup and olive oil and mix for a further 45 seconds to form a batter.

Spoon the batter into the prepared tin and smooth it out with the back of a spoon. Cover with well-oiled plastic wrap and leave in a warm, draught-free spot for 30 minutes to prove until risen by a third.

Meanwhile, sauté the bacon in a non-stick frying pan with 1 teaspoon olive oil for 5 minutes until lightly golden. Toss through the potato and cook for 5 minutes. Set aside to cool completely.

Remove the plastic wrap from the focaccia and drizzle the surface generously with olive oil. Press your fingers into the dough to leave indentations all over the surface, then press the garlic slivers into the holes and scatter the bacon, potatoes and rosemary over. Cover again with the oiled plastic wrap and leave to prove for a further 30 minutes until risen and bubbly.

Preheat the oven to 220°C/425°F (200°C/400°F fan-forced) with the oven rack positioned in the middle of the oven.

Once proved, remove the plastic wrap from the focaccia, drizzle the surface generously again with olive oil and sprinkle liberally with sea salt flakes.

Bake for 30–35 minutes until golden brown and crisp. Remove from the oven and leave to cool slightly before cutting. Scatter with more fresh rosemary leaves and serve warm.

TIPS

- While you can replace the buttermilk with water, it helps with the fluffiness of the focaccia and gives the bread a slightly sour taste that I find very appealing.
- Tossing the potatoes through the bacon coats the potato with oil so it cooks better on the focaccia, while pre-cooking the bacon gives it colour and helps make it lovely and crisp.

Cherry Tomato, Onion and Herb Focaccia

SERVES 8

Focaccia is back, baby! This classic Italian bread was on every Sydney restaurant menu in the '80s and now it's enjoying a resurgence. For good reason – chewy and crisp, it makes the perfect base for delicious ingredients such as tomato, onion and herbs.

2 cups (330 g/11½ oz) gluten-free plain (all-purpose) flour (see page 15 for recipe)

¾ teaspoon salt

¾ teaspoon gluten-free baking powder

2½ teaspoons instant dried yeast

1½ cups (375 ml/13 fl oz) buttermilk or water

2½ teaspoons rice syrup or raw caster (superfine) sugar

2 tablespoons olive oil, plus extra for drizzling

3 large garlic cloves, cut into slivers

½ onion, thinly sliced

1 cup (150 g/5½ oz) mixed cherry tomatoes, halved

2–3 oregano sprigs, leaves picked and finely chopped

2 thyme sprigs, leaves picked

sea salt flakes

Grease a 24 cm (9½ in) round cake tin or a 32 x 18 x 3 cm (13 x 7 x 1¼ in) brownie tray with olive oil.

Sift the dry ingredients into the bowl of a stand mixer with the paddle attachment fitted (or into a mixing bowl if using a hand mixer). Mix on low speed for 10 seconds. Slowly add the buttermilk, rice syrup and olive oil and mix for a further 45 seconds to form a batter.

Spoon the batter into the prepared tin and smooth it out with the back of a spoon. Cover with well-oiled plastic wrap and leave in a warm, draught-free spot for 30 minutes to prove until risen by a third.

Remove the plastic wrap from the focaccia and drizzle the surface generously with olive oil. Press your fingers into the dough to leave indentations all over the surface, then press the garlic slivers into the holes and scatter the onion, tomatoes and herbs over. Cover again with the oiled plastic wrap and leave to prove for a further 30 minutes, until risen and bubbly.

Preheat the oven to 220°C/425°F (200°C/400°F fan-forced) with the oven rack positioned in the middle of the oven.

Remove the plastic wrap from the focaccia, drizzle the surface generously again with olive oil and sprinkle liberally with sea salt flakes.

Bake for 30–35 minutes until golden brown and crisp. Remove from the oven and leave to cool slightly before cutting. Scatter with more fresh herbs and serve warm.

STORAGE
The focaccia will keep in the refrigerator in an airtight container for up to 3 days. Reheat before serving.

TIP
- I like to use plenty of fresh herbs on this focaccia, but dried herbs also work well. Just bear in mind that they are more pungent and should be used more sparingly.

Bacon, Potato and Rosemary Focaccia (page 204),
Cherry Tomato, Onion and Herb Focaccia (page 205)

Naan

MAKES 6

If you haven't had naan bread for a while because the good ones all contain gluten, you're in for a nice surprise. This leavened flatbread is soft, fluffy and delicious.

2 cups (330 g/11½ oz) gluten-free self-raising flour (see page 15 for recipe), plus extra if necessary

1 teaspoon xanthan gum

¾ teaspoon salt

1 teaspoon caster (superfine) sugar

2 teaspoons instant dried yeast

1 large egg, at room temperature

2 tablespoons softened butter or coconut oil

¾ cup (200 g/7 oz) Greek-style yoghurt or coconut yoghurt

2 teaspoons psyllium husk powder

¼ cup (60 ml/2 fl oz) water, at room temperature

1–2 teaspoons ghee or coconut oil, for cooking

STORAGE

Store wrapped in plastic wrap or in an airtight container at room temperature for 2 days. For best results, reheat before serving.

Sift the dry ingredients except the psyllium husk powder into the bowl of a stand mixer with the dough hook fitted (or into a mixing bowl if using a hand mixer). Mix on medium speed for 30 seconds. Slowly add the egg, butter and yoghurt and mix together for 30 seconds to form a dough.

Mix the psyllium with the water to make a slurry. Add to the bowl together with the yeast and mix for 90 seconds to combine.

Cover the bowl with plastic wrap and leave in a warm, draught-free spot to prove for 30 minutes, until risen by a third.

Turn the dough out onto a lightly floured surface and knead briefly until smooth, then roll out to form a log about 18 cm (7 in) long.

Cut the log at 3 cm (1¼ in) intervals into six equal pieces with a floured knife, then roll each piece out with a floured rolling pin into an oval approximately 3 mm (⅛ in) thick.

Heat a little ghee or coconut oil in a non-stick frying pan over high heat. Add a naan to the pan and cook until slightly charred and blistered on the underside, about 1 minute, then flip and cook for a further minute. Remove the naan from the pan and wrap in a tea towel (dish towel) to keep warm. Repeat with the remaining naan, adding more ghee to the pan as necessary, until all are cooked.

Serve warm with your favourite curry.

TIP

- To make garlic naan, simply spread ghee or clarified butter and 2 crushed garlic cloves over the top of each naan when you add it to the pan. Cook and flip it as before.

Roti

MAKES 8

By harnessing the magic elasticity of psyllium husk, you can enjoy the simple pleasure that is roti, an unleavened flatbread. It makes a perfect snack or accompaniment to your next Indian takeaway.

1 cup (160 g/5½ oz) chickpea flour (besan)

½ cup (85 g/3 oz) gluten-free plain (all-purpose) flour (see page 15 for recipe), plus extra if necessary

1 teaspoon psyllium husk powder

1 teaspoon salt

1 cup (250 ml/9 fl oz) boiling water

1 tablespoon light oil (e.g. sunflower), plus extra for cooking

Sift the dry ingredients into the bowl of a stand mixer with the dough hook fitted (or into a mixing bowl if using a hand mixer). Mix on low speed for 30 seconds. Pour in the boiling water and oil and mix for a further 30 seconds, until everything comes together to form a dough.

Turn the dough out onto a lightly floured surface and knead until smooth, then roll out to form a log about 16 cm (6¼ in) long.

Cut the log out at 2 cm (¾ in) intervals into eight equal pieces with a floured knife, then roll each piece out with a floured rolling pin into a disc approximately 2 mm (1/16 in) thick.

Heat a drizzle of oil in a non-stick frying pan over a medium–high heat. Add a roti to the pan and cook until slightly charred and blistered on the underside, about 1–2 minutes, then flip and cook for a further minute. Remove the roti from the pan and wrap in a tea towel (dish towel) to keep warm, then repeat with the remaining dough pieces, adding more oil to the pan as necessary, until all the roti are cooked.

Serve warm with your favourite curry.

STORAGE

Store wrapped in plastic wrap or in an airtight container at room temperature for 2 days. For best results, reheat before serving.

TIP

- Psyllium husk powder helps to form this dough, making it an essential ingredient in this recipe. Salt, meanwhile, is important for all bread recipes – it adds vital flavour and can help the bread rise.

Plain Bread

SERVES 10

Filling your home with the smell of freshly baked bread is easy with this simple recipe that anyone can follow, I promise you. Using a cast-iron casserole dish (Dutch oven) definitely gives the best results for baking bread. Once you are confident with this recipe, feel free to have a play with different flours you might prefer to use.

1⅔ cups (275 g/9¾ oz) gluten-free plain (all-purpose) flour (see page 15 for recipe), xanthan gum omitted

½ cup (60 g/2¼ oz) quinoa flakes

1 teaspoon salt

1½ cups (375 ml/13 fl oz) cold water

2 teaspoons rice syrup or honey

2 teaspoons olive oil

¼ cup (30 g/1 oz) psyllium husk powder

1½ teaspoons instant dried yeast

STORAGE

This loaf will keep stored at room temperature in a paper bag or wrapped in a clean dry tea towel for 3–4 days.

In the bowl of a stand mixer using the dough hook attachment, or in a large bowl if mixing by hand, add the flour (xanthan gum omitted), quinoa flakes and salt. Mix on low speed for 1 minute.

Add the water, rice syrup and olive oil and continue to mix on low speed for 5 minutes, then add the psyllium and yeast and mix on low speed for a further 5 minutes to form a dough. The dough will still be sticky, but it will come away from the side of the bowl if you use a spatula. Scrape the dough off the hook and let it sit in the mixing bowl for 5 minutes, so the psyllium can absorb all the liquid.

Turn the dough out onto a lightly floured surface. Sprinkle with a little flour and knead for 2–3 minutes to form a smooth ball.

Lightly flour a bamboo proofing basket or lightly oil a mixing bowl. Carefully place the dough in the basket or bowl with the smoothest side down. Cover with a damp tea towel and place in the refrigerator for 30 minutes.

Meanwhile, preheat the oven to 210°C/410°F (190°C/375°F fan-forced) with the oven rack positioned in the middle of the oven. Place a heavy-based deep cast-iron casserole dish with a lid (otherwise known as a Dutch oven) in the oven to heat.

Remove the dough from the refrigerator and tip out of the proofing basket onto a lightly floured bench. Score it with the tip of a sharp knife or razor blade, cutting a large 'X' in the top of the dough at least 1 cm (½ in) deep.

Remove the casserole from the oven, carefully place the dough inside, put the lid back on and return it to the oven. Bake for 45 minutes, then remove the lid and continue to bake for 25–30 minutes, or until the bread is golden with a nice thick crust.

Once cooked, turn the loaf onto a wire rack and leave to cool completely before slicing and serving.

TIP

- I prefer to use a lightly floured bamboo proofing basket to proof my bread. The dough doesn't stick, and it gives the bread a great pattern. Scoring the bread controls its expansion in the first part of the bake, so it doesn't rise in weird spots.

Seeded Bread

SERVES 10

Adding seeds to bread gives it a wonderful texture and taste. As with my plain bread recipe, this one is easy to follow, and you'll be delighted with the results. Your bread will stay moist for a few days at least.

1⅔ cups (275 g/9½ oz) gluten-free plain (all-purpose) flour (see page 15 for recipe), xanthan gum omitted

½ cup (60 g/2¼ oz) quinoa flakes, plus extra for dusting

1 teaspoon salt

1⅔ cups (420 ml/14½ fl oz) cold water

2 teaspoons rice syrup or honey

2 teaspoons olive oil

¼ cup (30 g/1 oz) psyllium husk powder

1½ teaspoons instant dried yeast

1½ tablespoons pepitas (pumpkin seeds)

1½ tablespoons sunflower seeds

1½ tablespoons linseeds

STORAGE

This loaf will keep stored at room temperature in a paper bag or wrapped in a clean dry tea towel for 3–4 days.

In the bowl of a stand mixer using the dough hook attachment, or in a large bowl if mixing by hand, add the flour (xanthan gum omitted), quinoa flakes and salt. Mix on low speed for 1 minute.

Add the water, rice syrup and olive oil and continue to mix on low speed for 5 minutes, then add the psyllium, yeast and seeds and mix on low speed for a further 5 minutes to form a dough. The dough will still be sticky, but it will come away from the side of the bowl if you use a spatula. Scrape the dough off the hook and let it sit in the mixing bowl for 5 minutes, so the psyllium can absorb all the liquid.

Turn the dough out onto a lightly floured surface. Sprinkle with a little flour and knead for 2–3 minutes to form a smooth ball.

Lightly flour a bamboo proofing basket or lightly oil a mixing bowl. Carefully place the dough in the basket or bowl with the smoothest side down. Dust with a few extra quinoa flakes, then cover with a damp tea towel and place in the refrigerator for 30 minutes.

Meanwhile, preheat the oven to 210°C/410°F (190°C/375°F fan-forced) with the oven rack positioned in the middle of the oven. Place a heavy-based deep cast-iron casserole dish with a lid (otherwise known as a Dutch oven) in the oven to heat.

Remove the dough from the refrigerator and tip out of the proofing basket onto a lightly floured bench. Score it with the tip of a sharp knife or razor blade, cutting a large 'X' in the top of the dough at least 1 cm (½ in) deep.

Remove the casserole from the oven, carefully place the dough inside, put the lid back on and return it to the oven. Bake for 45 minutes, then remove the lid and continue to bake for 25–30 minutes, or until the bread is golden with a nice thick crust.

Once cooked, turn the loaf onto a wire rack and leave to cool completely before slicing and serving.

TIP

- To make croutons, simply cut your bread (preferably 2–3 days old) with the crust on into whatever sized pieces you like. Place on a baking tray lined with baking paper and drizzle with olive oil, then bake in a 170°C/340°F (150°C/300°F fan-forced) oven for 20–25 minutes, rotating the croutons as you go, until golden. Remove from the oven and leave to cool before using.

GLUTEN-FREE BAKING MADE SIMPLE

THANK YOU

A huge thank you to my husband Peter and daughters Holly and Lucia, with whom I couldn't imagine life without. Thank you for being on this journey with me, and for letting me experiment with recipes on you. I always appreciate your honest feedback and your ongoing support and belief in me to keep me doing what I do.

Mabel, my mum, thank you for teaching me to cook from an early age, and for your endless support and help, particularly at the bakery. Thank you to Grace, my sister, who holds the fort at Wholegreen Bakery and works tirelessly and endlessly to make it all happen, to Kate and Justin my sister and brother-in-law for their unwavering support, and to Louise Hawson for her critique and magic through words and photos over the years at the bakery. Thank you to Coeliac Australia for their ongoing support and endorsement, and all the very special people that wrote a testimonial.

Thank you to Ben Dearnley, Vanessa Austin and Theressa Klein for creating and capturing the most delicious images I could ever imagine, to Emily O'Neill for the gorgeous design throughout these pages, and to Simon Davis, for your constant kindness and patience in editing. Thank you to Corinne Roberts, Jane Willson, Megan Pigott, Julie Mazur Tribe and Justin Wolfers from Murdoch Books who helped to make this book happen, and to my incredible staff whom I'm all so proud of.

And finally, to all of you that have helped to make Wholegreen Bakery what it is today. Without you, this book wouldn't have been possible.

ABOUT THE AUTHOR

Cherie Lyden is the founder of the beloved Wholegreen Bakery in Sydney. Having worked as a nutritionist and in food for many years, Cherie was diagnosed with hypothyroidism after her second child and then later with latent coeliac disease. Her youngest daughter was also diagnosed with coeliac disease at the age of four and then Hashimoto's disease at nine.

Passionate about food and despairing of the lack of good gluten-free food available – particularly baked goods such as bread, pastries and muffins – Cherie decided to start a bakery where everything tastes delicious, is made from scratch with real ingredients and no nasties, and is, importantly, 100 per cent gluten-free. Wholegreen Bakery now has three retail sites which are accredited by Coeliac Australia, and offers home delivery throughout New South Wales. Several varieties of Wholegreen bread, which are endorsed by Coeliac Australia, are available in supermarkets such as Woolworths Metro and Harris Farm Markets, as well as high-end restaurants, health food stores and cafés.

INDEX

A

almond meal
  dark chocolate and espresso cake
    with mascarpone cream 94
  lemon and coconut cake with
    lemon glaze 96
  lemon shortbread 68
  mixed berry frangipane tart 120
  pear and polenta cake with lemon
    and rosemary syrup 108
almonds
  apple, boysenberry and lemon
    crumble 72–73
  pear, blueberry and cinnamon
    crumble 72–73
  strawberry, rhubarb and vanilla
    crumble 72–73
Anzac biscuits 60
apples
  apple and cinnamon pie 128
  apple, boysenberry and lemon
    crumble 72–73
  blueberry, apple and lemon
    muffins 22
  fruit mince pies 130
asparagus: hot-smoked salmon,
  asparagus, pea and leek
  quiche 168

B

bacon
  bacon, cheddar, cherry tomato
    and chive muffins 145
  bacon, cheddar, onion and thyme
    quiche 164
  bacon, cherry tomato and basil
    scones 153
  bacon, potato and rosemary
    focaccia 204
bananas
  banana and maple buttermilk
    pancakes 77
  banana and pecan loaf 84
  banana, blueberry and coconut
    loaf 85
  banana, ricotta and honey
    muffins 25
  hummingbird cake with lemon
    cream icing and pecans
    102–103
barramundi, potato and fennel
  pie 173

basil
  bacon, cherry tomato and basil
    scones 153
  cherry tomato, feta, spanish onion
    and basil quiche 167
  mushroom, kale, parmesan, chilli
    and basil muffins 138
  peach and basil muffins 31
beef: slow-cooked beef and
  mushroom pies 180–181
berries. *See also* blueberries;
  boysenberries; raspberries;
  strawberries
  about 16
  mixed berry frangipane tart 120
biscuits
  Anzac biscuits 60
  chocolate chunk cookies 67
  gingerbread biscuits 62
  lemon shortbread 68
blueberries
  banana, blueberry and coconut
    loaf 85
  blueberry and lemon scones 55
  blueberry, apple and lemon
    muffins 22
  pear, blueberry and cinnamon
    crumble 72–73
boysenberries
  apple, boysenberry and lemon
    crumble 72–73
  vanilla, boysenberry and lemon
    cake with lemon syrup 113

breads. *See also* sweet breads;
  yeast recipes
  naan 208
  plain bread 210
  roti 209
  seeded bread 212
brioche 186
  dark chocolate brioche 188
  fruit brioche 187
  spinach and feta brioche 190
brownies, decadent dark
  chocolate 48
buns
  cheesy garlic pull-apart buns 200
  chocolate hot cross buns 196–197
  cinnamon pull-apart scrolls 199
  fruit hot cross buns 192–193
buttercream, vanilla 40
buttermilk
  bacon, cherry tomato and basil
    scones 153
  banana and maple buttermilk
    pancakes 77
  blueberry and lemon scones 55
  buttermilk pancakes 76
  buttermilk scones 53
  carrot and orange cake with
    cream cheese icing 99–100
  cheddar, corn and chive
    scones 152
  corn, green chilli and coriander
    buttermilk pancakes 158
  date, honey and thyme scones 54

fresh herb scones 150
roast pumpkin, parmesan and
    rosemary scones 157
vanilla, boysenberry and lemon
    cake with lemon syrup 113

C

cakes. *See also* cupcakes
    banana and pecan loaf 84
    banana, blueberry and coconut
        loaf 85
    carrot and orange cake with
        cream cheese icing 99–100
    dark chocolate and espresso cake
        with mascarpone cream 94
    decadent dark chocolate
        brownies 48
    hummingbird cake with
        lemon cream icing and
        pecans 102–103
    lamingtons 46
    lemon and coconut cake with
        lemon glaze 96
    lime, coconut and yoghurt loaf
        with lime drizzle 88
    pear and polenta cake with lemon
        and rosemary syrup 108
    sponge with strawberries and
        cream 107
    vanilla, boysenberry and lemon
        cake with lemon syrup 113
    zucchini and walnut loaf 90
carrot and orange cake with cream
    cheese icing 99–100
cheddar
    bacon, cheddar, cherry tomato
        and chive muffins 145
    bacon, cheddar, onion and thyme
        quiche 164
    cheddar, corn and chive
        scones 152
cheesecake, baked, with honey syrup
    and gingerbread crust 110
cheesy garlic pull-apart buns 200
chia seeds, about 16
chicken, leek, pea and tarragon
    pie 176–177
chickpea flour: roti 209
chilli
    corn, green chilli and coriander
        buttermilk pancakes 158
    mushroom, kale, parmesan, chilli
        and basil muffins 138
chives
    bacon, cheddar, cherry tomato
        and chive muffins 145

cheddar, corn and chive
    scones 152
chocolate and cocoa
    about chocolate 16
    chocolate chunk cookies 67
    chocolate hot cross buns 196–197
    dark chocolate and espresso cake
        with mascarpone cream 94
    dark chocolate brioche 188
    dark chocolate cupcakes with
        chocolate ganache 45
    dark chocolate, zucchini and
        hazelnut muffins 36
    decadent dark chocolate
        brownies 48
    lamingtons 46
    pear and hazelnut chocolate
        frangipane tart 122
    pear, dark chocolate and walnut
        muffins 30
    raspberry, white chocolate and
        coconut muffins 28
cinnamon pull-apart scrolls 199
cocoa. See chocolate and cocoa
coconut. *See also* coconut flour
    Anzac biscuits 60
    apple, boysenberry and lemon
        crumble 72–73
    banana, blueberry and coconut
        loaf 85
    lamingtons 46
    lime, coconut and yoghurt loaf
        with lime drizzle 88
    mango, lime and coconut
        muffins 34
    pear, blueberry and cinnamon
        crumble 72–73
    raspberry and coconut slice 50
    raspberry, white chocolate and
        coconut muffins 28
    strawberry, rhubarb and vanilla
        crumble 72–73
coconut flour
    dark chocolate and espresso cake
        with mascarpone cream 94
    lemon and coconut cake with
        lemon glaze 96
coffee: dark chocolate and espresso
    cake with mascarpone cream 94
cookies. See biscuits
coriander: corn, green chilli and
    coriander buttermilk pancakes 158
corn
    cheddar, corn and chive
        scones 152
    corn, green chilli and coriander
        buttermilk pancakes 158

cream cheese
    baked cheesecake with honey
        syrup and gingerbread crust 110
    carrot and orange cake with
        cream cheese icing 99–100
    hummingbird cake with lemon
        cream icing and pecans
        102–103
crème pâtissière, easy 126

crêpes 78
    See also pancakes
crumbles
    apple, boysenberry and lemon
        crumble 72–73
    pear, blueberry and cinnamon
        crumble 72–73
    strawberry, rhubarb and vanilla
        crumble 72–73
cupcakes. *See also* muffins
    dark chocolate cupcakes with
        chocolate ganache 45
    lemon cupcakes with lemon
        glaze 42
    vanilla cupcakes with vanilla
        buttercream 40

D

dairy and non-dairy equivalents,
    about 16
date, honey and thyme scones 54
dill
    barramundi, potato and fennel
        pie 173
    hot-smoked salmon, asparagus,
        pea and leek quiche 168
    spinach and feta brioche 190

spinach, feta, cherry tomato and
  dill muffins 136
dried fruit
  fruit brioche 187
  fruit hot cross buns 192–193
  fruit mince pies 130

E

eggs
  bacon, cheddar, onion and thyme
    quiche 164
  cherry tomato, feta, spanish onion
    and basil quiche 167
  hot-smoked salmon, asparagus,
    pea and leek quiche 168

F

fennel: barramundi, potato and
  fennel pie 173
feta
  cherry tomato, feta, spanish onion
    and basil quiche 167
  roast sweet potato, zucchini, feta
    and rosemary muffins 141
  spinach and feta brioche 190
  spinach, feta, cherry tomato and
    dill muffins 136
flour blends, homemade gluten-free
  plain flour 15
  self-raising flour 15
focaccia
  bacon, potato and rosemary
    focaccia 204
  cherry tomato, onion and herb
    focaccia 205
fruit crumble 72–73
fruit mince pies 130

G

ganache, chocolate 45
garlic pull-apart buns, cheesy 200
gingerbread biscuits 62

H

hazelnuts
  dark chocolate, zucchini and
    hazelnut muffins 36
  pear and hazelnut chocolate
    frangipane tart 122
honey
  baked cheesecake with honey
    syrup and gingerbread
    crust 110
  banana, ricotta and honey
    muffins 25
  date, honey and thyme scones 54

gingerbread biscuits 62
hot cross buns
  chocolate hot cross buns 196–197
  fruit hot cross buns 192–193
hummingbird cake with lemon
  cream icing and pecans 102–103

K

kale: mushroom, kale, parmesan,
  chilli and basil muffins 138

L

lamingtons 46
leeks
  barramundi, potato and fennel
    pie 173
  chicken, leek, pea and tarragon
    pie 176–177
  hot-smoked salmon, asparagus,
    pea and leek quiche 168
lemons
  apple, boysenberry and lemon
    crumble 72–73
  blueberry and lemon scones 55
  blueberry, apple and lemon
    muffins 22
  hummingbird cake with lemon
    cream icing and pecans
    102–103
  lemon and coconut cake with
    lemon glaze 96
  lemon cupcakes with lemon
    glaze 42
  lemon shortbread 68
  lemon tart 125
  pear and polenta cake with lemon
    and rosemary syrup 108

vanilla, boysenberry and lemon
  cake with lemon syrup 113
lentils: French lentil, spinach and
  sweet potato pie 172
limes
  lime, coconut and yoghurt loaf
    with lime drizzle 88
  mango, lime and coconut
    muffins 34
linseeds: seeded bread 212

M

mango, lime and coconut
  muffins 34
maple syrup: banana and maple
  buttermilk pancakes 77
mozzarella: cheesy garlic pull-apart
  buns 200
muffins. *See also* cupcakes
  bacon, cheddar, cherry tomato
    and chive muffins 145
  banana, ricotta and honey
    muffins 25
  blueberry, apple and lemon
    muffins 22
  dark chocolate, zucchini and
    hazelnut muffins 36
  mango, lime and coconut
    muffins 34
  mushroom, kale, parmesan, chilli
    and basil muffins 138
  nectarine, orange and thyme
    muffins 35
  peach and basil muffins 31
  pear, dark chocolate and walnut
    muffins 30
  raspberry, white chocolate and
    coconut muffins 28
  roast sweet potato, zucchini, feta
    and rosemary muffins 141
  spinach, feta, cherry tomato and
    dill muffins 136
  zucchini, caramelised onion,
    parmesan and thyme
    muffins 140
mushrooms
  mushroom, kale, parmesan, chilli
    and basil muffins 138
  slow-cooked beef and mushroom
    pies 180–181

N

naan 208
nectarine, orange and thyme
  muffins 35

O

onions
  bacon, cheddar, onion and thyme
    quiche 164
  cherry tomato, feta, spanish onion
    and basil quiche 167
  cherry tomato, onion and herb
    focaccia 205
  zucchini, caramelised onion,
    parmesan and thyme
    muffins 140
oranges
  carrot and orange cake with
    cream cheese icing 99–100
  nectarine, orange and thyme
    muffins 35
  strawberry, rhubarb and vanilla
    crumble 72–73
oregano
  cherry tomato, onion and herb
    focaccia 205
  fresh herb scones 150

P

pancakes. *See also* crêpes
  banana and maple buttermilk
    pancakes 77
  buttermilk pancakes 76
  corn, green chilli and coriander
    buttermilk pancakes 158
parmesan
  cheesy garlic pull-apart buns 200
  mushroom, kale, parmesan, chilli
    and basil muffins 138
  roast pumpkin, parmesan and
    rosemary scones 157
  spinach and feta brioche 190
  zucchini, caramelised onion,
    parmesan and thyme
    muffins 140

parsley: fresh herb scones 150
pastry
  savoury dairy-free shortcrust
    pastry 163
  savoury decadent shortcrust
    pastry 162
  sweet dairy-free shortcrust
    pastry 119
  sweet decadent shortcrust pastry
    116–117
peach and basil muffins 31
pears
  pear and hazelnut chocolate
    frangipane tart 122
  pear and polenta cake with lemon
    and rosemary syrup 108
  pear, blueberry and cinnamon
    crumble 72–73
  pear, dark chocolate and walnut
    muffins 30
peas
  barramundi, potato and fennel
    pie 173
  chicken, leek, pea and tarragon
    pie 176–177
  hot-smoked salmon, asparagus,
    pea and leek quiche 168
pecans
  banana and pecan loaf 84
  hummingbird cake with lemon
    cream icing and pecans
    102–103
pepitas: seeded bread 212
pies. *See also* tarts
  apple and cinnamon pie 128
  barramundi, potato and fennel
    pie 173
  chicken, leek, pea and tarragon
    pie 176–177

French lentil, spinach and sweet
    potato pie 172
  fruit mince pies 130
  slow-cooked beef and mushroom
    pies 180–181
pineapple: hummingbird cake with
    lemon cream icing and pecans
    102–103
plain flour, homemade gluten-free 15
polenta: pear and polenta cake with
    lemon and rosemary syrup 108
potatoes
  bacon, potato and rosemary
    focaccia 204
  barramundi, potato and fennel
    pie 173
pumpkin: roast pumpkin, parmesan
    and thyme scones 157

Q

quiche
  bacon, cheddar, onion and thyme
    quiche 164
  cherry tomato, feta, spanish onion
    and basil quiche 167
  hot-smoked salmon, asparagus,
    pea and leek quiche 168
quinoa
  Anzac biscuits 60
  plain bread 210
  seeded bread 212

R

raspberries
  raspberry and coconut slice 50
  raspberry, white chocolate and
    coconut muffins 28
rhubarb: strawberry, rhubarb and
    vanilla crumble 72–73
ricotta
  baked cheesecake with honey
    syrup and gingerbread crust 110
  banana, ricotta and honey
    muffins 25
rosemary
  bacon, potato and rosemary
    focaccia 204
  fresh herb scones 150
  pear and polenta cake with lemon
    and rosemary syrup 108
  roast pumpkin, parmesan and
    thyme scones 157
  roast sweet potato, zucchini, feta
    and rosemary muffins 141
roti 209

S

scones
  bacon, cherry tomato and basil scones 153
  blueberry and lemon scones 55
  buttermilk scones 53
  cheddar, corn and chive scones 152
  date, honey and thyme scones 54
  fresh herb scones 150
  roast pumpkin, parmesan and thyme scones 157
scrolls, cinnamon pull-apart 199
seeded bread 212
self-raising flour, homemade gluten-free 15
shortbread, lemon 68
shortcrust
  savoury dairy-free shortcrust pastry 163
  savoury decadent shortcrust pastry 162
  sweet dairy-free shortcrust pastry 119
  sweet decadent shortcrust pastry 116–117
slices
  decadent dark chocolate brownies 48
  raspberry and coconut slice 50
smoked salmon: hot-smoked salmon, asparagus, pea and leek quiche 168
sour cream
  savoury decadent shortcrust pastry 162
  sweet decadent shortcrust pastry 116–117
spinach
  cherry tomato, feta, spanish onion and basil quiche 167
  French lentil, spinach and sweet potato pie 172
  spinach and feta brioche 190
  spinach, feta, cherry tomato and dill muffins 136
sponge
  sponge cake for lamingtons 46
  sponge with strawberries and cream 107
strawberries
  sponge with strawberries and cream 107
  strawberry, rhubarb and vanilla crumble 72–73
  strawberry tart 126
sunflower seeds: seeded bread 212

sweet breads
  brioche 186
  chocolate hot cross buns 196–197
  cinnamon pull-apart scrolls 199
  dark chocolate brioche 188
  fruit brioche 187
  fruit hot cross buns 192–193
sweet potatoes
  French lentil, spinach and sweet potato pie 172
  roast sweet potato, zucchini, feta and rosemary muffins 141

T

tarragon: chicken, leek, pea and tarragon pie 176–177
tarts. *See also* pies
  bacon, cheddar, onion and thyme quiche 164
  cherry tomato, feta, spanish onion and basil quiche 167
  hot-smoked salmon, asparagus, pea and leek quiche 168
  lemon tart 125
  mixed berry frangipane tart 120
  pear and hazelnut chocolate frangipane tart 122
  strawberry tart 126
thyme
  bacon, cheddar, onion and thyme quiche 164
  cherry tomato, onion and herb focaccia 205
  date, honey and thyme scones 54
  fresh herb scones 150
  nectarine, orange and thyme muffins 35
  zucchini, caramelised onion, parmesan and thyme muffins 140
tomatoes
  bacon, cheddar, cherry tomato and chive muffins 145
  bacon, cherry tomato and basil scones 153
  cherry tomato, feta, spanish onion and basil quiche 167
  cherry tomato, onion and herb focaccia 205
  spinach, feta, cherry tomato and dill muffins 136

V

vanilla
  vanilla, boysenberry and lemon cake with lemon syrup 113
  vanilla cupcakes with vanilla buttercream 40

W

walnuts
  carrot and orange cake with cream cheese icing 99
  pear, dark chocolate and walnut muffins 30
  zucchini and walnut loaf 90

X

xanthan gum, about 16

Y

yeast recipes
  bacon, potato and rosemary focaccia 204
  brioche 186
  cherry tomato, onion and herb focaccia 205
  chocolate hot cross buns 196–197
  dark chocolate brioche 188
  fruit brioche 187
  fruit hot cross buns 192–193
  naan 208
  plain bread 210
  seeded bread 212
  spinach and feta brioche 190
yoghurt
  lime, coconut and yoghurt loaf with lime drizzle 88
  naan 208

Z

zucchini
  dark chocolate, zucchini and hazelnut muffins 36
  roast sweet potato, zucchini, feta and rosemary muffins 141
  zucchini and walnut loaf 90
  zucchini, caramelised onion, parmesan and thyme muffins 140

Published in 2023 by Murdoch Books, an imprint of Allen & Unwin

Murdoch Books Australia
Cammeraygal Country
83 Alexander Street
Crows Nest NSW 2065
Phone: +61 (0)2 8425 0100
murdochbooks.com.au
info@murdochbooks.com.au

Murdoch Books UK
Ormond House
26–27 Boswell Street
London WC1N 3JZ
Phone: +44 (0) 20 8785 5995
murdochbooks.co.uk
info@murdochbooks.co.uk

For corporate orders and custom publishing, contact our business development team at
salesenquiries@murdochbooks.com.au

Publishers: Corinne Roberts and Jane Willson
Editorial Managers: Julie Mazur Tribe
and Justin Wolfers
Design Manager: Megan Pigott
Designer: Emily O'Neill
Editor: Simon Davis

Production Director: Lou Playfair
Text © Cherie Lyden 2023
The moral right of the author has been asserted.
Design © Murdoch Books 2023
Photography © Ben Dearnley 2023
Cover photography © Ben Dearnley 2023

*Murdoch Books acknowledges the Traditional Owners of the Country on which we live and work.
We pay our respects to all Aboriginal and Torres Strait Islander Elders, past and present.*

ISBN 978 1 92261 617 3

A catalogue record for this book is available from the National Library of Australia

A catalogue record for this book is available from the British Library

Colour reproduction by Splitting Image Colour Studio Pty Ltd, Wantirna, Victoria

Printed by Hang Tai Printing Company Limited, China

IMPORTANT: Those who might be at risk from the effects of salmonella poisoning (the elderly, pregnant women, young children and those suffering from immune deficiency diseases) should consult their doctor with any concerns about eating raw eggs.

DISCLAIMER: The information and suggestions in this book are for your consideration only and may not be suitable to your particular circumstances. We are not recommending that people eat certain foods or follow any particular dietary advice. This is particularly so if you have allergies or other conditions that may give rise to adverse reactions to certain foods or diets. Before undertaking any of the suggestions in this book, therefore, we strongly recommend that you consult your own health care professional. Neither the author/s nor the publisher accepts any liability or responsibility for any loss or damage suffered or incurred as a result of undertaking or following any suggestions contained in this book.

OVEN GUIDE: You may find cooking times vary depending on the oven you are using. This book uses fan-forced ovens. For conventional ovens, as a general rule, set the oven temperature to 20°C (35°F) higher than indicated in the recipe.

TABLESPOON MEASURES: We have used 20 ml (4 teaspoon) tablespoon measures. If you are using a 15 ml (3 teaspoon) tablespoon add an extra teaspoon of the ingredient for each tablespoon specified.

10 9 8 7 6 5 4 3 2 1